SHINE
Your
BEACON
BRIGHTER!

*When Darkness Tries to
Snuff Out Your Light*

LINDA SOMERS

Published by Elite Foundation®, Fort Lauderdale, Florida
Book Cover: Jesus Cordero
Literary Mentor and Editorial Review: Dr. Jessica Vera, PhD

Elite Foundation® is a registered trademark

Printed in the United States of America.
Hardcover ISBN: 978-1-7320778-9-8

This publication is designed to provide accurate and authoritative information regarding the subject matter covered. It is sold with the understanding that the publisher is not engaged in rendering legal, accounting, clinical or other professional advice. If legal advice or other expert assistance is required, the services of a competent professional should be sought. The opinions expressed by the authors in this book are not endorsed by Elite Foundation and are the sole responsibility of the author rendering the opinion.

Most Elite Foundation® titles are available at for bulk purchases for sales promotions, premiums, fundraising, and educational use. Special versions or book excerpts can also be created on direct request for specific needs aligned with Elite Foundation®

For more information, please write:
Elite Foundation® Publisher
1451 West Cypress Creek Road, Suite 300, Ft. Lauderdale, Florida 33369
Or email: ElitePublisher@EliteFundsFreedom.org
Visit us online at: www.EliteFundsFreedom.org/book_program

Elite Foundation is a 501(c)(3) nonprofit organization that offers Indie publishing services to impact lives and community. When you Invest in Yourself, you Fund Freedom. Royalties from all our goods and services support scholarships/grants and the work done with victims and survivors of human exploitation and sex trafficking. Elite Foundation's vision is to eradicate the aftermath experienced by victims by co-creating a future for every survivor.

TABLE OF CONTENT

DEDICATION

I dedicate this to my mother Carmela Somers,
the true Beacon light in my life...
Whom always helped me navigate through the darkness...
I love you.

FOREWORD

There are moments in life that are defining, this is undeniable particularly at this moment in human history. We are in the middle of a global pandemic. The world is battling a virus that has influenced every single human being on this planet. This shared experience is not unlike the experience of pain, it too is universal.

The negative energy of our current human circumstance in 2020 can be extremely dark and heavy, if left to be significant. However, the author, Linda Somers share her life philosophy and how the simple things, like kindness, compassion, and gratitude can lift the spirit, no matter the circumstance. She prefers to focus on others in the chaos, and to know that her Light is here to impact those who have yet to find theirs.

Linda Somers has experienced her share of significant pain and loss in her life, but this extraordinary woman's actualization journey is testimony to all that can be accomplished when there is courage to act in faith with joy.

At times in her life, even the thought of sharing her story was an impossibility due to the residual impairments from her multiplicity of ailments, injuries, and pain. Yet here it is. Linda Somers has persevered against many odds and through the refinement process has gained such practical wisdom and maturity that you would think would take a few lifetimes to learn, if ever.

The beauty of this literary work is that Linda Somers shares her learnings so that other people do not have to experience the same hardships. However, if they do, Linda's red flag system ensures that the possible blind spots are fully lit and seen. Her life experiences have not been in vain, quite to the contrary, they have allowed her to evolve into the woman, professional and humanist she is today.

It is evident from this work that Linda Somers' purpose is not egocentric, but other centered. This read is a must for everyone and particularly at this time in human history. There is a substantial need to use the global pause we have all been experiencing to fully appreciate our life and all the details it contains that make up who we are and how we are to impact the world.

Congratulations to Linda Somers for a dream realized and for a life well lived!

Onward and upward, Warrior-Sister.

Dr. Jessica Vera, Ph.D.

Elite Foundation

CHAPTER 1

THE EARLY YEARS

———————

I believed I had a 'normal' childhood till age five at least, nothing out of the ordinary happened that I recall. But when I turned six-or-seven-years old things dramatically changed because I remember that I started having some serious nightmares. Just so you know, unlike how kids grow up today, watching everything possible on screens with the reality shows and movies leaving little to the imagination, I didn't watch horror movies or read anything that could put negativity into my mind. I was raised very sheltered from the real world. I was not exposed to much 'darkness', at least not early on.

The nightmares though were unlike anything that I had seen on television, they were vivid and involved being abducted by aliens. In them were my mom and my dad, that is until I woke up in my dream, but in reality I was not awake. They still were like these aliens, apparently, that's what my imagination made my parents look like in my mind. I have reflected on these nightmares for years. I am now in my fifties and it has taken decades for me to be able to share my truth from what these vivid images in my head revealed.

In the nightmares, the alien was not himself; he was obviously on drugs, alcohol or whatever else they were into at the time. For the longest time, I could not see the face or make out the identity of the alien. Now I know that the nightmares that haunted me for years, they were how my brain sorted out things that were happening to me, but I could not deal with that at the time. These pictures in my head were how I survived and suppressed my trauma memories for so many years. But they would resurface every so often. This is how I know that at a young age I went through emotional situations that affected my trust of others and my belief that someone who loves you can still hurt you.

I also remember that it was because of these nightmares that I always wanted to sleep with my mom during those years. It is funny to me how from within my nightmares, I would wake up a few times, but still be dreaming, and I'd feel afraid to go back into a deep sleep. I do not believe that I was really afraid of the nightmare, but rather of just going back to sleep and what could happen to me whilst in that state.

There are chunks of memories from my childhood that I do not fully understand, but what I can share is that everything (nightmares/emotional distress) kind of stopped when the use of drugs and alcohol in the house stopped being part of the issue. It was also at that same timeframe that we moved to Coral Springs, Florida and my life changed. Things seemed to improve, but there was a new challenge.

By this point, I was now a tall, lanky, skinny, and buck-toothed preteen who was very awkward and always felt out of place, I truly felt very different from others my age in some way. The differences did not bode well in middle and then high school. During those years, I was a bit of an outcast. I had a hard time making friends. I had a couple of good friends from elementary thru high school, But at 16 It was with one of my so-called 'friends' that I trusted that I would be led into an experience I'd never wish on my worst enemy.

This girl asked me to go with her and these two guys that I did not know, it seemed at the time, innocent enough. We went out into the field. But the entire time while walking I wondered, "What is going on with me? I felt nervous and scared." I did not understand why I was feeling this way until that trusted friend left me with the unknown guy, and he took me to a car. It is still difficult to share what happened, but it's important that you know. It was a very scary situation that was totally blocked from my mind because he made me do things that I had never done before. He forced me to have sex with him and forced himself onto me to have oral sex with him as well. The experience shaped how I used to feel about sex. The guy, who raped me, told me that he would never let me out of the car and that if I said anything about what he did, he would tell everyone in the school. I did not know who he was, so I did not know what he was capable of doing. I attended a school with a student body of over 2,000 kids. He told me he would make sure that everyone knew that I was a "slut." He bullied and intimidated me to have sex. I had never spoken of it, until now.

It really did not matter though, because even though this secret was kept locked deep within, I would end up being bullied anyways by teenaged mean girls, just about how different I was. In those days I tried to be friends with everyone. I tried to never be part of a clique. I tried helping others and to get along with everyone. I guess I was somewhat of a peacekeeper. I always tried to help others because "I think nobody was ever around to help me. I was never protected or felt safe. So, I know firsthand how important that provision for others can be." This is my 'Why' for my mission today. It is to make others feel safe, protected and that they can trust me. My approach did not make a difference as a teenager though, because I was the brunt of everyone else's ridicule. It was a difficult time in my life.

You might be wondering where my parents were as all of these experiences were happening to me. My mother has always been my everything. My mom is my best friend to this day. She has always been by my side. My mom had me late in life, at 35 and in the midst of a busy season in her own life. As I'm writing this, I'm recalling that she did know about my rape as a teenager. Actually, she is the only one who knows about everything. She just did not know what to do for me, except to be present, which meant everything to me.

> I LEARNED EARLY
> IN LIFE THAT JUST
> BEING PRESENT IS SO
> IMPORTANT.

I learned early in life that just being present is so important. You have to be present for people when they need you because that is exactly what I never had happen in my early years, and as we continue down this journey, you'll read that it has been a theme throughout life.

The bullying at school escalated over time, my mom tried to help me, and my teachers did also. As a matter of fact, I had a good relationship with my school dean. I made good grades and my mom even got me braces and I knew it was a sacrifice because we did not have the money for them. My mom did everything she could to help me feel more confident and to help me fit in. Today, when I reflect it seems so pathetic to think that outward appearance gives people value and the ability to fit in. I completely loved my mom for trying so hard to help me. I still remember how she would say, "Linda hold your head up high." I would tell her, "I can't, if I lift my head up, they will harass me even more [because I was so much taller than most of the girls in school]." Of course, now I know better, "Hold your head high indeed!"

School was a challenging place to be as a teen, and my home life, well to give you an idea of the tension, I knew that I was either the problem or maybe the reason why my parents stayed together. Being the baby of the family, I believe my parents stayed married, unhappily, to financially secure my life. Not that we lived in extravagance, but a single parent would have really struggled. Even so, we never went on family trips or did anything as a family. My siblings were eight and 10 years older than me, they had different family experiences than me. By the time I came into the family, things were vastly different, we led a very separate lifestyle. My mom and dad barely spent time together. I do not remember eating meals together with my dad, Mom always had dinner ready for all us siblings to join at the table. My dad worked really long, late hours and he traveled a great deal as well. I was always aware of the tension between them. I knew how much my mother resented and despised my dad and I always knew it was because of me that they stayed together. This caused me to develop an unshakeable feeling of guilt that I have carried for years.

When people say that they stay together for their kids, I always think to myself, you do not realize what you are doing to the kids. My family experience did not give me a good foundation of what a healthy marriage or family life should be, because I never witnessed or lived it. I know that my siblings may disagree with my perception of our home life, but for me, it is my truth. There was no seen love, compassion, holding hands, respect or anything loving between my parents. Consequently, I never really learned in childhood what love looked like and sex well that was another total misunderstood part of life for me, because of all the hurt that it caused me in my younger years. To me, intimacy and sex were just ways to control and hurt (both physically and emotionally). That was my family context. Just know that despite all that I have shared about my family life, it did not take away from the fact that I loved my dad and adore my mom.

One other fact I need to share, right after my rape experience and amidst my season of bullying, a Memorial Day holiday fast approached. This holiday would cause me even greater pain still yet. My father stayed home from work for the holiday, I was home, and my brother was outside working out. Nobody else was home, my mother was out shopping. Everything was good when out of nowhere, my father started gasping for air on the couch. I started screaming, "Help, help, help!" I knew to call 911 and after I did, I started hitting my dad to get him to react. My brother then came running in and he tried to perform CPR on our dad and my dad sat up. He sat up straight. Where was I, you're thinking? I was sitting behind my dad supporting his body up and holding him, as best that I could. He said, "What's wrong? What is wrong? I'm fine." His eyes were wide open, and he looked perfectly fine. I said, "Oh thank God he's fine." But within seconds, he fell right back down into my arms. The ambulance finally arrived. At the time we lived in the westside of the city and it took a long time, at least that is how it seemed, like forever for the ambulance to arrive. By the time it did, I was screaming in the middle of the street, "Hurry, hurry..." They took my dad away in the ambulance, that is after they worked on him in front of me, while I was hysterical, seeing his body be jolted in the air as they shocked him with the paddles and rushed him out. I was left sitting on the floor alone and numb. When my mom came back home, that is how she found me. My mother and brother had gone with our dad in the ambulance. Hours later my brother returned home. He ran into the house and threw a glass against the wall screaming, "He's dead. He's dead." This is my last memory from that time period. I seriously cannot remember anything else about those years.

Afterwards, I learned to work a great deal to pay for my own car, insurance and whatever else I needed to get to work and school. I also remember I didn't leave much time for anything else. My grades, I kept them up, that is except for darn history. That class messed me up, but funny enough I love history now and I now live in a historical mini castle from the 1920s but back then it was my nemesis.

The bullying at school...well that continued to escalate. During one incident a girl put a knife to my throat while she was calling me a "whore, slut, bitch." you name it, I was called it. Between all of that, my rape, and the death of my father, it is no wonder I only have sketchy memories from those days.

In my early years, I was invisible most of the time, I did get noticed, but only by those I least desired the attention from...the mean girls. I made sure to stay afloat though, I left little time for anything else. But, to my surprise, I did end up dating one guy, my best friend at the time. He was different from all the other guys. He was awesome. A real good guy, but he had his own host of problems with his family being extremely religious and cruel towards him. He ended up moving in with my family when he turned 16. We dated for a bit, then he and his family reconciled and relocated to Texas. His leaving broke my heart. We tried the long-distance thing for our senior year, but phone calls were not enough.

My best friend gifted me the first positive experience with a guy, and this led to a false sense of security. I thought, "Maybe not all guys are bad?". That is when I convinced myself to give it a try, I started giving relationships a chance and became infatuated with a guy, older, by two years at the time, a co-worker. I was always so nervous to even look at him or to speak to him. I felt I was a silly giddy awkward girl with no confidence, and he was cute. He was tall, dark-haired with amazing blue eyes. He was my dream guy, I was taken by the tall, dark, and handsome guy, but the attraction did not last long. I learned even back then, people can be all looks on the outside but inside, ugh. I did not actually date him long enough to figure it out, but I learned quickly he was all about himself. So, I ended it.

During a birthday party sometime later, I met another guy, Brian. Brian used a stupid line to attract me and it worked, his quirky silliness got me smitten and he too was a tall and blue-eyed blonde cutie pie. Brian, at least I could talk to, but I felt so shy around him also, I just did not have confidence. Brian was a Florida Gator; I would travel up to Gainesville often to visit him but quickly realized he was a party boy and that he flirted with everyone.

This was my season of learning about different types of guys. I also started working in a clothing company and to my surprise, Brian would find out where I was working and would show up unannounced. These little encounters, I have to admit, did boost my self-confidence a little. Brian was a little late though because I had already met another guy, who I would eventually make my husband. Actually, when I told Brian about John [my prince charming], and that I could not date him, Brian asked me to marry him. Brian was a big joker, so I never took him seriously and besides, he was a lady's man. I ran from potential pain and betrayal and chose to move forward with John.

It's funny, even though the years leading up to this point in my life were horrific in many ways, as I've shared, there were those who saw me as, "Oh you're beautiful. This, that and whatever else they thought that gave them permission to dislike me and to bully and hurt me." To myself, I was a flat-chested, boyish, tall girl who was always being ridiculed but who also was walking the modeling runways in Miami. I was modeling for magazines and in the beauty industry, but I never believed it myself. I just did not really bloom or grow up until way later in life.

I was an extremely late bloomer.

CHAPTER II

BLOOMING DUCKLING
MEETS PRINCE CHARMING

———

*I*t takes a lifetime to grow and understand oneself. To really know your inner self-worth and to have beauty on the inside, which is most important. I believe I was always beautiful on the inside, but instead of manifesting it outwardly towards people, mostly because people hurt me early on, I channeled my love towards animals. I love stray and injured animals and I have a way with them that heals. Even as a young child I would cuddle the little ducks out by my house and the mama duck would bring her babies to my screen every day, so that I could pet and cuddle them. It's that unconditional and untainted love that is pure.

Through some personal work, I have learned about my personality type. When you start learning and understanding yourself from the inside out, it all starts to make sense. I just wish that my current self could have told my past self that it was all going to be okay. Just love yourself.

> **JUST LOVE YOURSELF**

The reality though is that it was hard for me because I was being abused and used at the time. After I was raped these negative self-concept feelings even got worse. The tragedy of the untimely death of my father just compounded my negative self-concept because I thought, "He didn't love me more than his cigarettes and they killed him."

I started dating John at 19. He was the family member of a next-door neighbor. I knew him for a while before we got married. But we were both incredibly young. John was a sweet 19-year-old, charming and charismatic guy. We moved in together within a month. I was the financial provider in the relationship working two and three jobs. John did not speak English, I had to teach him. He learned and then he started working, but in the interim, we lived off my income and credit. John was Latin and was used to being taken care of by his mother, who he was trying to get away from. Or so I initially thought. It was not long before I learned that John was actually also trying to get away from a child that he conceived and denied paternity to, back in his native country. I was a perfectly innocent target. A magnet for dysfunctional relationships, because I was attracted to men that I thought I could help and fix. John had a cute accent; a nice smile and he was fun. We went everywhere together, trips, dancing, clubbing. We did something every weekend for many years of our marriage. But slowly I lost my friends, as I became more and more isolated. John did not like spending time with my family which led to my estrangement from them, as well. This left just him and I all the time.

I have learned that those with a narcissist personality try to isolate their partner because they can easily abuse them without outsider involvement when they accomplish it. John was a charmer. If there were people around, he would turn it on, but I soon would come to learn the other side of John's behavior behind closed doors. It might sound as though I regret this relationship, there are things about it that were very painful, but I also learned a great deal about who I am, and how I can survive just about anything because of my marriage to John.

Now 23, and four years into my marriage, I had become the awkward, withdrawn and timid child once more, due to the unrelenting scolding from my husband. John would get upset by the slightest things like the faucet head being set to hot. There was a list of things he didn't like, and he made sure that I knew every single one of them. He often would say to me, "I should only have to ask once…". Our marriage of 22 years was a living hell for most of it. I tried truthfully to be the loving, attentive wife but if I asked anything of John that didn't involve going on expensive trips or buying luxury items, he would conveniently be unable to do it and somehow made it my fault. I started feeling sick inside most of the time, because honestly at the time, I did not understand what was going on in my household, except that I could do nothing right. And worse, he would often compare me to his mother, who I later learned he despised. It got to the point that I started to resent myself because I was not able to stand up for myself. You might be wondering, "Weren't there warning signs?".

Yes, now in hindsight I see things clearly, but back then, I didn't. He did disclose that he was a bully in high school and his admission that I would not have liked him back then should have been a bull horn warning. Or my experience when his sister moved in with us and he basically allowed her to stay without any sharing of costs. My sister-in-law was a disastrous mess and she created that physically in our house as well. She would use all my laundry supplies and had no consideration for me or even her brother. It got so bad living with her that I had to say something and when I did, John told me, "I'm not going to choose between my sister and you, and if you don't like it, you get out." It was a clear tell sign, but I guess somewhere deep inside I believed that I deserved to be treated so poorly. It was obvious that John had no respect or love for me. He and his sister were just using me.

The abusive relationship was a challenge, but it was around the same time when I started to experience some health problems. Initially, no one knew what was wrong with me. I was attending college, had just bought us a house and furnishings with my credit. From the outside in everything looked picture perfect. I had always been very financially responsible. I had a great credit score and I always took care of the finances because John did not know how. Financial responsibility is one of the gifts I gained from my early traumatic loss, and the need to work. There was no other choice in my world. My father had died in my arms when I was so young and left me in the care of a single parent with limited resources. I had to be responsible and take care of myself.

There is a little something that I still carry about this responsibility thing…you see my father was a smoker and he was told to quit. He chose to continue smoking and till this day, I still believe he chose cigarettes over me. Not to mention that when he died, he left no insurance or saving. We were renting and my mom had to get a minimum paying job because she had been a homemaker the better part of her adult life. This led me to start working at age 16. I worked two jobs and then worked another job with a course called DECA. By the time John came into my life, I had a high credit score, bank account and savings, as well as a car. Likely John saw in me a young financially responsible person. In hindsight, these types of men prey on strong independent women or young adults, because they want to feed their ego by tearing us down. They want to snuff out our light. He accomplished it for a number of years in my life because every encounter with John led to the depletion of my self-esteem. I know what you are thinking now, "Why did I stay in the marriage so long?".

The answer…because I was depleted.

My body was starting to shut down, with increasing health issues that would result in 22 different surgeries. I do not doubt that unresolved emotional issues and stress had a lot to do with waking up my disease or rather, causing my brain to hemorrhage. I have an intolerance to stress even today if my blood pressure rises it can cause a bleed. I have a rare and debilitating disorder with a familial genetic predisposition. But, for now, stay with me, I was just trying to survive, to go to school and to pay my bills, all while keeping a clean pristine home to make my husband, John happy. Of course, an impossible feat.

My health, my needs, etc. they never came into the realm of consideration not even for myself back then. Not unlike my younger years, I did not matter. But what did matter was the education my parents gave me about how to cohabitate without actually being engaged with one's spouse. I mirrored them well, staying married because it was the thing to do. Besides, I was not a quitter. Marriage was supposed to be forever. I tried to communicate with John, but I only got rejection from him. Did I mention, I was also still modeling as one of my many resources generating side gigs. John never attended any of my fashion shows. He would not because it would mean the possibility of being outshined. It was part of his duty to keep me down, humble, under his control.

My health continued to deteriorate, and it was as though it favored John because it meant that I was physically weak, and he had power over me. I was dependent on him at times for the simplest of self-care activities. And he took full advantage of this power position.

My very bubbly, happy and silly girl disposition saved me. My mother warned me never to lose that special part of me and I have held on tight. I lost many things through my marriage, friends, resources, and time, but I kept my disposition. I also maintained a relationship with John's mother, even though he really did not want me to. John had "real bad mother issues." God forbid his mother called and I answered the call and passed along the telephone to him, he would curse me out for doing so. But, with a sleight of hand, he would be all sweet towards his mother on the phone. It was so blatantly obvious the split personalities, but there was little I could do then.

When I first met John, he told me about a child he had in Columbia and that the child was two or three years old. I told him then, "Oh my God, well let's adopt her and bring her here." He was like, "No, no, no. I don't want kids. I'm too selfish. I'm too narcissistic and selfish to want kids. I want to travel." I do not know why but "I should have believed him then." It's crazy thinking about this because obviously, John knew he was narcissistic even back then. I am talking 30 years ago now. We were married for twenty-five years, in all. When he told me about his child, I insisted that we bring the child to the US, but he opposed me and told me that the mother of his child was a "whore, slut and crazy, a drug addict." He tried to convince me that the child might not even be his because of the mother's promiscuity. Now on the other side of this relationship, I have learned that this type of personality will blame others and will project and gaslight the other person to glorify themselves. At the time, John let his mother believe that I was the one keeping him from his child in Columbia. It took me 25 years to tell my mother-in-law the truth. I have to admit when I was finally able to share that truth with her, it made me feel better, and also, I was able to tell her that I was the one sending the gift packages to the child all the time, John did not want to do so.

This reconciliation of truth with my mother-in-law created more problems in my marital relationship because John was running away from Columbia when he met me, and I was starting to make him have to face his responsibilities. I was all in favor of reuniting the child with us and forming a family with her here in the USA, but John wanted nothing to do with it. He was really clear that he did not want to raise a child. After 20 years of battling this issue with John, I learned that his daughter at 18 or 19, ended up on the street, all drugged up on cocaine and got hit by a car. She survived but needed a blood transfusion. It was this incident that proved John's paternity and prevented him from denying his responsibilities to his child any longer. This affirmation of paternity led to an improved relationship between myself and John's family, but this did not last long because John was able to manipulate them, and they eventually cut all ties with me.

The only obvious joy John experienced in our marital relationship was when he was buying something big like a car or house or something like that or planning a trip. We traveled a lot because that was the only way he was happy and nice to me.

However, without a missed beat the day before returning from whatever trip, John would always start a fight with me to reset the power differential in our relationship in his favor. He would behave and say horrible things out of nowhere, and I would be completely caught off guard. This is gaslighting, it leaves you thinking, "Wait what just happened." To give you an example, he would start a fight over the sky being purple when it was blue.

> THIS IS GASLIGHTING, IT LEAVES YOU THINKING, "WAIT WHAT JUST HAPPENED."

This would lead to a drown out argument and insults in abundance about me being less-than and needing medical help. The incidents escalated exponentially throughout our relationship and they left me walking on eggshells all the time and in survivor mode for almost 25+ years of my young adult life.

CHAPTER III

JEKYLL AND HYDE

---

*A*fter living through half of my life in emotional and physical pain in a marriage to a seemingly Prince Charming, but actually to a man with a narcissistic personality, it warranted its own chapter in my journey. Not because of anything personal, but rather because I do not want another woman to have to live through 25 years of hell in a marriage that is destined to destroy itself and you in the process. I am not a psychologist; these are just my experiences and what I've learned from my own healing journey through therapy.

How do you know if a person has a narcissistic personality disorder?

Firstly, you have to know that it is a mental condition, "In which people have an inflated sense of their own importance, a deep need for excessive attention and admiration, troubled relationships, and a lack of empathy for others. But behind this mask of extreme confidence lies a fragile self-esteem that's vulnerable to the slightest criticism."

A narcissistic personality disorder causes problems in many areas of life, such as relationships, work, school, or financial affairs. People with a narcissistic personality disorder may be generally unhappy and disappointed when they are not given the special favors or admiration they believe they deserve. They may find their relationships unfulfilling, and others may not enjoy being around them. That is not what is difficult, I was enamored by John at first and he was so very charming, just what every woman would want in a man. I didn't find it difficult to be around him until it was too late, and I was already married a few years, and he had gotten us into substantial financial distress.

The Symptoms of Narcissistic Personality Disorder

- Have an exaggerated sense of self-importance
- Have a sense of entitlement and require constant, excessive admiration

- Expect to be recognized as superior even without achievements that warrant it
- Exaggerate achievements and talents
- Be preoccupied with fantasies about success, power, brilliance, beauty, or the perfect mate
- Believe they are superior and can only associate with equally special people
- Monopolize conversations and belittle or look down on people they perceive as inferior
- Expect special favors and unquestioning compliance with their expectations
- Take advantage of others to get what they want
- Have an inability or unwillingness to recognize the needs and feelings of others
- Be envious of others and believe others envy them
- Behave in an arrogant or haughty manner, coming across as conceited, boastful, and pretentious

> HAVE AN INABILITY OR UNWILLINGNESS TO RECOGNIZE THE NEEDS AND FEELINGS OF OTHERS

- Insist on having the best of everything — for instance, the best car or office

At the same time, people with a narcissistic personality disorder have trouble handling anything they perceive as criticism and they can:

- Become impatient or angry when they do not receive special treatment
- Have significant interpersonal problems and easily feel slighted
- React with rage or contempt and try to belittle the other person to make themselves appear superior
- Have difficulty regulating emotions and behavior
- Experience major problems dealing with stress and adapting to change
- Feel depressed and moody because they fall short of perfection
- Have secret feelings of insecurity, shame, vulnerability, and humiliation (Mayo Clinic)

Why does it take so long sometimes to really see the personality characteristics by somebody?

Normally, it can take four to six months before a person will detect symptoms and characteristics of a narcissist, but it is not an exact science. When my marriage started imploding, I started seeing therapists to deal with my husband's behavior and I was told by the therapists that he likely had a type of narcissistic sociopathic disorder. This started me on a quest to research and to learn all I could. I read consistently that there were known signs. I saw the signs, but it took me a long time to really believe that what I was living through with John was actually signs of narcissism.

Once I learned of the signs, I was stuck in it. I did not understand what narcissism was 25 years ago like I do now. Now, I can see the red flags flying left and right and it's been hard to date because I see them right away.

Twenty plus years ago, you just never heard about that type of thing. You're just wondering "What the heck? I always thought he was bipolar." I called him Jekyll and Hyde because one minute, he would be okay but then he would turn on a dime. It was just like I said, walking on eggshells constantly. I was always sick to my stomach and stressed out. Even for the little things, I would always have to be home by 5:30 and have dinner on the table by six because he just made it where if I didn't, I knew what I would have to deal with afterwards. I just tried to always please him and to do everything right. I figured if I did everything right, maybe, just maybe, he would be nice. Maybe, just maybe, he would be the good John and not the bad. I would do everything I could to keep him on the good side and not the evil side. It did not matter how much I did. The more I did for him, the more I was creating a monster and losing my life, independence and who I was. I was just catering to him constantly. Down to even if I came home say five minutes late, so my car would be a little warm to the touch of the hood, and this would lead him to start in on me.

Does any of this sound familiar?

Everything is your fault right. That is gaslighting.

Then comes the alienation from others. John tried to put distance between my mother and I, but he never accomplished it. I think that he may have had two conversations with my mother in the 25 years we were married. Also, he would call my mom Carmela, even though he knew she hated Carmela. She liked Millie. It just was so weird and so cold dealing with him and my mother. He never called her Mom. But despite all of his active efforts, he was never able to separate us. My mother is the only one who ever saw the real state of my marriage. And that is because I so wanted to have the perfect marriage and the perfect life. You just try to think "Well, things will get better. He's just having a bad day." I do not like to sit and complain to anybody, especially not in my family. While they think everything is wonderful because we are going on trips and buying houses and cars. All that material stuff, which in the long run, I learned later in life means absolutely nothing. The reality was something quite different. Apart from my mother though, John did manage to alienate me from every friend or acquaintance I had.

Then once they have you without a support system, the fights begin to escalate. John would have fights planned from the moment the slightest thing was not to his liking. If I left the facet turned to hot or my car engine was a little warm, then it would trigger an all-out fight. These types of fights were constant, daily. I was the type of wife that would go and put on a little dress, put a little makeup on even if I were sick as a dog. Because the last seven years of our marriage, I was in and out of so many surgeries that I did not work. The first 15 plus years, I did. I worked my two, three jobs and went to college. I still tried keeping the house, keeping the dinner on the table at the right time, doing everything. Just so much stress and anxiety but I knew I was better. I knew I could do more. I knew that this was not the life that I wanted, except when he was having a good day. That is the rollercoaster ride they take you on. You're thinking "Well, maybe he is going to change. Maybe he isn't as bad as I'm feeling." I would start to put that doubt in my head, but they do that. They know how to manipulate and put doubt into your mind and into your soul. To start making you not believe your own reality and cause you internal confusion. Every day was just extremely tough.

When I first started getting my brain hemorrhages and I was in and out of the hospital two times a year, at least a week or two weeks at a time having bleeds, he was not so bad then. He was helpful in the hospital. He was helpful in front of people but then when I got home and I really needed the help, it was behind closed doors and I could not move, this is when he would ignore me. Now I was an inconvenience. There were several times where I was paralyzed. I absolutely could not move and had to use the bathroom for example, and it would create an all-out war of words about pitch and tone etc. John knew that I needed him for the basics, but he did not care. Without a limited support system, my poor mother couldn't do everything. John was my husband and would not listen to my needs. He would purposely walk away while I was talking to cause me to raise my voice, then he would scold me for raising my voice, all while leaving me in need to use the bathroom. At times, it would get so frustrating that I'd pull my hair out because of not being able to make sense of the new reality he had created for me. John loved to mock me and "ooh your poor little victim" to make me feel like a victim. Then without notice of any kind, he would switch and be sweet, attentive to my immediate needs and this constant switching in behavior led me to believe that maybe there was something wrong with me. Maybe I was not loud enough when I asked for help, or maybe I was too loud. What I can share is that this led my health to deteriorate further, and he seemed to become happier the weaker I was.

At the time, I was not strong enough to end the marriage.

I wasn't strong enough to answer back.

I wasn't strong enough to tell people anything.

He knew he had me captive, basically captive in our home. That is why when people say, "How did you stay so long?" I tell them it was because you are in daily emotional survival mode. And, in my personal case, I was also dealing with health issues that led to a multitude of surgeries and repeated hospitalizations. As if the deterioration of my health was not enough at the time, I also was involved in a few accidents. A poll fell on me at a department store and it split my wrists apart. This led to four surgeries and casting of both of my wrists just before we left on a trip that John had planned to Ireland. We were going for a month and it did not matter to him that I couldn't use my hands, I just had to grin and make the best of it, so that I did not set him off. I also broke my neck in a car accident. The silver lining for John, this provided a cash settlement that allowed him to indulge in buying car after car, but I made sure we still had enough in savings. Yet another tactic used by abusive spouses they create financial stress.

The seemingly unending stress of my marriage and the toll it took on my body, health and soul were so devastating at the time. But I would come to find out that although painful, the life lessons it taught me would shape who I would become. I learned that I did not want to survive my marriage, I wanted to survive, period!

It is amazing to me, even to this day how people can be deceiving. I married Prince Charming, but quickly I learned that John had another side. A dark side that I never even thought could be possible. But, it was very real, and it caused us both a great deal, even though he might have thought that he got away with everything that he wanted, in the end that was not the truth.

Bullies gaslight even within a family...

Remember my childhood bully, she is now my sister-in-law. Her one plight in life has been to ostracize my brother from the family. In her eyes, my family is problematic, dysfunctional even and the worst part is my brother has bought into her lie. He does not get along with the rest of the family. For a period, there, she had even managed to keep me from my sister. There have been many antics perpetrated by this woman.

She once created a plot against my eldest brother, who has done nothing but support almost everyone in our family at one time or another. My brother was married 40 years ago, when I was still a young child. Fast forward to a few years ago, a woman by the name of Mary and my last name accidently sent me a message through my social media. I later learned her message had been intended for my sister-in-law. My bully and her husband (my other brother) had created a conspiracy theory to undermine my eldest brother and it almost worked.

One of their other plots did work and till this day, I'm still grappling with how they could do it to my mother. Somehow, during a moment of vulnerability, they convinced my mother to take out a twenty-five-thousand-dollar loan for them. They had no intention to pay it back and my mother does not have the resources to satisfy the loan. They would have gotten away with it were it not for my mother breaking down crying and telling her other three children of the plot. I know that was difficult for my mother, and that if there were a way for her to keep quiet about it to avoid conflict with her son, she would have.

I'll never understand how people can be so manipulative and hurtful even to their kin. But then again, I was married to a man who had me convinced he was Prince Charming and took over 25 years of my youth.

People's true self eventually gets unmasked. I just wish that we did not have to go through so much pain in the process of their unveiling.

CHAPTER IV

MY SAVING GRACE

---

*I*n the midst of all the chaos of my bad marriage and the multiple medical procedures for various health issues, it was discovered that I had a rare condition. A genetic disorder that I would find out later was the cause of my father's death, and the reason for which I continue to live.

> **THERE IS ALWAYS A SILVER LINING IN THE MIDDLE OF CHAOS. YOU MIGHT NOT SEE IT RIGHT AWAY, BUT IT WILL BE REVEALED TO YOU WHEN ITS CRUCIAL.**

If it had not been for the multitude of tests I had to have during the early stage of finding out what was going on with me physically, I might not be writing this book for you today.

There is always a silver lining in the middle of chaos. You might not see it right away, but it will be revealed to you when its crucial.

My reveal came when I was found to have a tumor. During one of my hospitalizations, I had to have an MRI and the results revealed cavernous angioma inside my spinal cord at the T-11 level of my spine. The physicians were baffled by the findings, so they ordered more tests.

And whilst still in the middle of the stress of not knowing what was wrong with me, I ended up with a brain bleed. This landed me in the hospital for several weeks. During that time, I underwent thorough testing and my husband had to be on his best behavior. By all the testing, the physicians did rule out having multiple sclerosis, but they were unable to provide me with a clear diagnosis or treatment. At the time it was explained to me that I had varicose veins in my brain and spinal cord. They were all tangled and knotted, and bleeding and the physician explained that they did not understand why. I found myself in the middle of it all doing research again, but this time it was for myself. This was before Google was simple. Back then, you could not just ask Bixby or ask your computer, "Hey, what is this?" It took a long time to do a lot of research, not like today. Today, Google knows all.

My search led me to find a hospital in Germany by just typing in varicose veins in the brain and how to strengthen varicose veins. I learned how to change my diet and eat right. What to drink, what not to drink, what kind of vitamins would strengthen my veins. I did a detox with a nutritionist. I just started to figure it out. I told myself, "Well, if these doctors can't help me, I'm going to help myself." This doctor in Germany happened to pop up. I said, "Well, I wonder if I can talk to somebody over there?". Once I confirmed that I could speak with them, I asked my German speaking neighbors to help me with translation on the call. After I explained my condition and situation, I was put in connection with a physician who was studying a similar case in Switzerland. I was able to get a hold of this doctor in Switzerland and he advised he was being transferred to Duke University to continue as a professor and neurosurgeon. When he did, he took me on as a patient.

Ultimately, my medical case became part of a research study being completed by Duke University and Mayo Clinic. While in the process, I met a woman, Connie, who had just started an organization called Angioma Alliance (angiomaalliance.org). That organization utilized the research of my case and that of

Connie's daughter, as we were the first known cases of this disorder. Connie's daughter was a baby at the time of going through the brain hemorrhages, so I became the guinea pig. We found out that the disorder is based upon a mutated inherited gene. One of my brothers had the mutation but was asymptomatic. My other two siblings do not have the mutated gene. This meant that either my mom or dad had it. We were able to confirm that my dad had the disease and it likely killed him. The reason we know he was the one we inherited it from, is because his brother had it and we know Mother was tested and did not have the mutation. However, being a familial gene mutation and a 50/50 chance of a child getting it, it had to have been my dad. The good thing is that my siblings who had kids, do not have it. So, they are safe, and their kids are safe. My eldest brother and I did not have kids so that was a good thing, because we would have had a 50/50 chance of our kids inheriting the mutated gene and disorder. My unique disorder requires that I adhere to regular testing and follow-up. I have had in excess of 62 MRIs in my life thus far. In resume, I am what you could call a scarred woman, literally, I have had four wrist surgeries, a pelvic surgery, and ten (10) back surgeries (because an implanted stimulator put up into my brain ended up getting infected and I developed a staph infection). The infectious disease doctor became a regular person in my life, as I had to have follow-ups with the physician every other day for a year in order to fight the infection. I could not believe everything I went through, but I was not going to be taken down by an infection. I was like, "You've got to be kidding me." It was dangerous. It looked like things were not going very well. Then after about a year, I finally kicked it.

Shortly after that, I had to have brain surgery and luckily so, because I had several bleeds. In fact, I had two cavernous angiomas and one aneurysm that needed to be cut out of my brain and if any had ruptured again, they would have taken me out. I remember not being able to even put a children's puzzle together after the brain surgery. I remember the noises were so loud after the surgery because my hearing overcompensated for my loss of vision, that thank goodness, even though the vision impairment is permanent at least the hearing and loud noises was temporary.

I remember one of my first outings after brain surgery, which of all the surgeries I have had this one scared me most and I created documents for everyone in my family. I updated my will with details of who would take care of my home, fish, pets and especially Chewy… the CDs I made everyone was to tell each and everyone how much I loved them and a bunch of pictures etc… I was scared about this surgery. It was also during this surgery experience that my brother actually said he loved me before I abruptly was pulled into pre-op and watched my mother crying. It was the first time that I thought I might not see them again. Shaking and crying hysterically, I asked to be given medication to knock me out. Instead, nurses came out to try and cheer me up dressed as clowns. I hate clowns but I knew they were trying to help and I kind of even chuckled and said, "I hate clowns" and we all laughed. You know who I did not even think of…John.

I awoke after the surgery and I did recognize John, Mom, and my brother and the first thing I did was smile …. then puke. They gave me the wrong meds for the puking, and I had a seizure. Then a few hours later I tried to awake again… I smiled and phew, no puking. The recovery period could begin. I had to relearn everything, even seeing differently because my spatial perception was affected, and I saw what was like a mirage in my vision field. When I described it to my brother, he said, "It's like you're on mushrooms." That is how I used to explain it to my neurosurgeon, "My brother said this area of the brain is where people tripping on mushrooms are affected." The doctor said, "Yeah. That's about right." I said, "Was that why everything looked like a mirage?". He said, "Yes." To the left, my area of perception is just all like a mirage effect on the left side and then down. Because I do not see a quarter of my vision from my right eye and three quarters of my vision on my left, my perception remains permanently off.

I always knock things out of people's hands. I try to understand walking downstairs, how far the stair is, it is not the same as how everyone else sees things. It took so long to understand and learn and relearn how to walk and how to walk downstairs and how to stop, focus, look, and pay attention. Look down, use your right eye, just a toll on things that I had to learn over again. It took a long time. I

> HOW TO WALK DOWNSTAIRS AND HOW TO STOP, FOCUS, LOOK, AND PAY ATTENTION

had an open craniotomy. The open craniotomy, they took the scalp of my hair off. At least I was able to save some of my hair.

They sutured the hair and they glued it back on with nuts and bolts and plates in my head to hold everything together.

After all that, just seven months after the brain surgery, they found a spinal cord tumor that was inside the cord and that was a possible bleed. I was being warned that I was going to have to have the spinal cord surgery and/or just be paralyzed when it bleeds. At least the spinal cord surgery could give me a chance at possibly walking. I was hoping for longer than seven months though in between it and the brain surgery. At that point, I just remember not having too much in the way of family support, they just did not understand. I still think to this day they might have thought I had Gamma Knife and not open brain surgery. One of my siblings came up to me and hit me on the head and said, "Hey, kiddo. How are you doing?". I was like, "Oh," with my walker and just sitting there like, "Oh, my goodness. Oh, my goodness." I am assuming she just did not understand what was going on. I was just flabbergasted. Granted, we were not too close at the time, but I did not think it was that bad. I always reached out to help her and to do everything I could for her because of her issues and problems with her pregnancies. I would always bring chicken noodle soup over to her house and just make sure everything was okay when she was sick. I would bring baskets of herbal cough drops and herbal everything when she was pregnant to make sure she did not do anything wrong. She did have a lot of miscarriages, which I understand was horrible for her.

When I needed my family the most though, I really did not have them. I had my mother and I really had the support of my older brother. Other than that, at that time, there was a big distance between the siblings. It was just getting worse and worse because I guess apparently to them, I was told I was taking too much of our mother's attention. When a sick sibling is down, of course, a mother and everybody should gather around that sick sibling. Just like I would do, or anyone would do in that situation. You gather around and lift them up and not hold them down. It was not quite like that with my family.

Just seven months after the brain surgery, my spinal cord bled, and I was on the couch. I just could not move. I did not know who to call or what to do. I was shaking. I knew I had my angel flight ready and the plane ready if I needed them to take me, etc. I knew the spinal cord was bleeding. I was having difficulty walking, breathing, etc. I did not want to call my mom because at her age and the stress, I didn't want to put it on her. I knew my sister was working right down the street from me. I figured let me call her. I said, "My spinal cord is bleeding. I can't feel my legs. I'm on the couch." She said, "Hold on, kiddo." I was holding and I was holding, and I was holding, and I am shaking and shaking. I had just had brain surgery, so I was not supposed to be stressing out. I was on the couch crying and shaking. "What do I do? What do I do?". The phone said 18 minutes I was holding. In the meantime, I had a friend call me from high school that I had not seen for 10 years but she just reached out feeling like something was wrong. She was right, something was horribly wrong. She was the one that got into her car and drove to my aid immediately. She drove a half hour from her house to me and came to my rescue. In the meantime, as she is driving, my phone is clicking. I said, "Well, let me get that my sister's calling. Maybe she's sorry." When I answered the phone, she goes, "When is your surgery?" She heard me. I said, "Now, immediately. I got to go now." I was shaking and crying. She said, "Well, mom's going to have to go after because I already am on the calendar to go to the Bahamas and she's supposed to babysit for me." I'm like, "No.

She's going to want to go with me. She's not going to drive eight hours by herself. She doesn't drive 95 first of all." But I insisted, "She's going to have to go with me. She's not going to want her daughter just after brain surgery alone knowing what the doctor told me, she knew I could be paralyzed. We're just going to cross our fingers and hope that I get some of it back. I knew what kind of surgery I was going in for, so did my mother." My sister was like, "Well, no. She's going to have to go after. She's got to babysit for me." I was like, "No, no, no. She's going to want to be with me." She just said, "Yeah, I'm sure," and hung up on me. I never talked to her again for many, many years after.

Thankfully, I not only survived the surgery, but regained most of my mobility. But the recovery and rehabilitation were really hard and to this day, I have physical and perceptional impairments from it, and I have had to endure several other procedures since. It is funny how people closest to you can actually challenge whether or not you are truly experiencing what you are going through.

Throughout the years, during holiday gatherings, I would have family members actually tell me and others that they did not believe me and thought that everything was just made up stories to gossip about amongst the family. And yet others, who might have witnessed the one occasion when my husband lifted me up from my wheelchair to try to have me dancing, was proof to them that I was faking it and was not disabled at all. The truth is, that the entire ordeal of wanting me to dance with him, was excruciating for me, but like usual, I did what I could to please him. Afterwards, it took me about two weeks to recover from the bursitis and excruciating pain of those few minutes of supported movement. Someone recorded it though and sent the recording to the Social Security Office to challenge my disability. I later learned it was actually one of my relatives and it was heart-wrenching for many years to know this fact. The other way that the family hurt me was that they ostracized me from celebrating Christmas or holidays and when they did come around me they would mock me by saying, "Does she look paralyzed to you?". That video was shown to visiting relatives and it resulted in my total alienation from the family. During this time in my life, I was not only being tormented at home by my husband, but now my family members were emotionally bullying me as well. I felt so isolated and this was perfectly wonderful for my husband.

My family thought that I had a happy perfect marriage because they did not know what was going on behind closed doors. Actually, they never got involved or cared about me enough to want to find out. The exceptions, my mother and my one brother.

Another family stress at the time was that we were all dealing with my grandmother's dementia and her need for daily support. It was just a horrible time to be in the wheelchair, just trying to survive. I was told later that apparently the spinal surgery was more brutal than expected and longer than expected. They had to cut the spinal cord open at three levels. They told me that I would never walk again. I was like, "No, no, no. that's not going to happen. I am going to do this." But the nerve pain was excruciating. They call it phantom pain because if I didn't see my legs, I didn't feel them. Till this day, this holds true. I don't feel my legs if I don't see them.

Imagine, you don't feel your lower body, whatever is to the left of me I don't know about because of the impairment caused by my brain surgery and just to add insult to injury, if I'm not in pain, then I'm in complete numbness because not all of my organs function as they should. When I share greater details of all my physical issues with people, I see the sheer disbelief in their faces. I am a walking miracle. I know and this is why I felt I needed to share my story, because obviously all of these experiences have happened for a reason.

It was an exceptionally long four-year recovery period. I went to physical therapy every single day. I had a little service dog with me after the brain surgery that stayed with me the entire time, his name is Chewy. He and my mom accompanied me during this period. I learned later that my family had an issue with my mom's involvement in my therapy as well. Apparently, they questioned why my husband wasn't the one taking me to rehabilitation. Ironically, during this time in my marriage, my husband had to work to pay all the bills. In actuality, he financially supported us the last seven years of our marriage.

I have often been asked what triggered the downward spiral of your marriage?

I have pinpointed that the one thing that started us on the path to the end of our relationship was when he had to start pulling his own financial weight in the household. He was used to being taken care of, not the one having to be taking care of me. That escalated the riffs in our relationship even though I still did everything I could for him. I continued to make his meals, by bracing myself up out of the wheelchair as best as I could to get dinner on the table when he expected it.

My life routine revolved around going to therapy every single day in excruciating pain. Getting up into the therapy apparatus to try to get my brain to remind my body how to move my legs. The machines were awesome, amazing. I had the best of everything because of the great fortune to be a Duke University research subject. My progression to give you an idea was to go from mechanism, to a wheelchair, to then walkers, and then to rolling walkers to get into a chair. I eventually progressed to the Cadillac of walkers. It had brakes and everything, so I was able to even walk an aisle or so at Publix. That would be my exercise. I would sit down after taking a few steps. Every step I took was the most amazing accomplishment in total pain. I wore Size 11 men's shoe because my feet and legs were so swollen. From what the nurses and doctors told me, to give you a further visual, my pain was similar to the pain experienced by a burn victim. The tighter the shoe, the more compressed. I had to be in a compression sock or shoe, then the nerve pain would not be so bad. I would always really wear tight snorkel shoes and socks. No one could go near my feet when I did not have on tight snorkel shoes. I lived and slept in those things. I did everything in them, I showered in them because I am like, "Oh, my gosh." The water is so painful and cold air and rain, still very, very painful to this day. There are certain different levels of nerve pain that I had to learn to deal with every day. Then to my amazement, I went from my Cadillac walker to forearm crutches without the slightest help from John. He found that he was no longer the center of my attention because my body became that for me.

I learned to walk again through my amazing experience of therapy. My rehab was similar to what amputees have to go through. They would push me over, so I'd learn how to get up with my good right thigh. Also, how to engage my hips correctly because my hips were good, and my right thigh was good. That gave me the chance that I could beat my circumstance. Little by little I moved forward a little bit at a time.

You know what remains a chilling memory even today - waking up from the spinal cord surgery and being told, **"You will never walk again."**

I proved them wrong.

It took many years to figure it all out, but I stopped fainting when upright. Those early emotional memories of what it felt like, how can I explain them. It was like floating and I did not understand why I was floating. It is just the most awkward feeling. You know that you are upright, but you do not feel your lower body. You can see it in your reflection in the mirror, but you do not feel it. It was mirror training that was used to reconnect my brain with my physical movement. Even though I did not feel it, my brain computed what I saw in the mirror and I started to make progress. I always had a mirror in front of me for all my therapies and all my training. Everything I would do I would always have a mirror. Still to this day, when I am walking in an area that I don't know or where there's curves and bumps and things that I don't know, I have to be careful and see my surroundings. Of course, walking in my own home, I understand my home. I know it inside and out. I feel comfortable in my home. It's like a blind person in their own surroundings. I have the visual deficits, but I also have the leg deficits and the balance issues. Simple tasks like walking and talking to someone could be dangerous for me because I am visually distracted. Boom and I can collapse. Every step I take, I have to think about it. When I was in therapy at St. Mary's Hospital for months and months, in my head, I would sing the song, "You put one foot in front of the other and soon you'll be walking out the door." I would sing that song every single day through therapy. It would just get me going and make me giggle. I always kept that positive attitude because what else was I going to do?

'WHAT ELSE YOU CAN DO STEMS FROM FINDING A ROUTINE OF ACTIVITIES AND ACTIONS THAT PROMOTE AND MOTIVATE YOU TO MOVE FORWARD ONE STEP AT A TIME.'

What else you can do stems from finding a routine of activities and actions that promote and motivate you to move forward one step at a time. I know this today.

Every morning, one thing I would do was make sure that I woke up with opera playing on my earphones. It was just something that gave me chills through my whole body. I felt like I could feel it down to my toes even though I could not feel my toes. It is like I felt it through my whole body. What is funny is that specialists would come and go, each tried different techniques and modalities to try to get me to feel something, acupuncture for example but I just didn't feel it. Instead what I felt most had nothing much to do with my physical abilities, but rather a great deal more to do with my ability to maintain my positive disposition, even when everything was bleak. In those days, you would find me rolling around the hospital bringing cake to everybody on the ward who was bed-bound.

I remember one of my birthdays spent whilst in the hospital. My girlfriend brought me a birthday cake and set it and all types of decorations, balloons, and everything else, up in a room, as a surprise. It was still such a hard time for me in recovery. I was on very heavy doses of medication and I did not tolerate narcotics well. They would make me throw up and I just could not eat. Irrespective when I got wind of what my girlfriend had done for me, I wanted so badly to enjoy her surprise. I went on my wheelchair over to the room. She had all this beautiful food. Everything was gorgeous. I was just like, "Oh, my God.

That is so nice. No one's ever done this for me." This is the same friend that came to my rescue the day I had to be rushed in for emergency spinal surgery and my sister refused to come over and kept me on the phone on hold. I was so thankful to have this woman in my life. She was there by my side throughout my hospital stay and beyond. I really wanted to enjoy my birthday with her. However, as soon as I saw the food, in one second, I was like, "I got to go back to the room." I wheeled back to the room and started throwing up. I felt so bad. They gave me the Phenergan and before I realized it I was out. I apparently was out for two to three hours before I woke up again and everything was still as my friend had set it up.

After I woke up I told myself, "Well, I couldn't enjoy my birthday cake but let's put smiles on everyone's face." The nurses cut up the cake for me and I rolled around the stroke floor because I was on the stroke and the rehab floor for paralysis. The man next door to me, he had lost his leg in a motorcycle accident. Another person had a stroke. Everyone had some neurological deficit on the floor. I rolled around and I'm like, "Birthday cake. I got birthday cake." Everyone is like, "Oh, I'll have a slice." I just felt so good to just bring happiness and smiles to everybody. I said, "Oh, you know what? This is something I want to always do. I always want to just make people happy." I remember going by this one room and the man hadn't spoken. He had a stroke. He hadn't spoken the whole time up until that point. As I wheeled by his room the nurse said, "Well, no. He hasn't said a word since his stroke." I heard someone in the room mumble, "Cake?" I go, "Nurse, nurse. He just said cake. He just said cake." I was so excited. The nurse was like, "What? Really?". She went into the room and the man said cake again. It was carrot cake so there were little nuts in it. The nurse just smushed up a little piece of the carrot cake and a little bit of the icing and fed it to the man. It was his first words and his first little bite of something other than the mushy foods that they had been giving him. I was so excited I could not wait to tell my girlfriend, Tatiana what joy your birthday cake brought to everybody on that floor. I said, "That's it. This is what I've got to do." Once I left the hospital and fully returned home, I made the decision to become a Mentor for the Brain and Spinal Cord Institute of Florida. Ironically, during the acute time between my brain and spinal cord surgeries, John was somewhat decent.

In the hospital, he was fine. In front of doctors, he was fine. In front of family, he was fine. But when we got back to his life and his world then the expectation started again. I guess he expected that I would jump back to it, being his wife. He thought that I would be all better, but then he started asking, "What's wrong with you?" and he would lose his patience with me. To him now I was only an inconvenience. I am not hard to deal with. I was always joking and bubbly. I was always trying so hard and working my ass off. I am not one of those woe is me people who go and sit in the corner and sulk. I maintained a positive attitude. I was in fight mode.

I called him the mean nurse because I could not get out of bed. I had to ask for help. That is when he would always yell at me and make me stop asking. The more I would ask for anything, the more I would be getting yelled at. I would just sit there. I would hold it and hold it and hold it. I ended up having a pee-pee bag, so I did not have to ask him. It was just terrible. If I needed my medication or water, I would suffer to not ask him for help. These are the things that I experienced and that had me questioning at the time,

"Why did I do that?

Why did I put up with that?

Why? Why? Why? I should have, could have, would have."

You know what?

I am never going to say should have, could have or would have again because I learned. I learned from those experiences and it set me up to live better the next half of life. The next 50 years of my life I am going to be a completely different person. Instead of regret, now I say what I need to say, of course in a kind and warm way because I am not a mean person, but I am never ever going to just not help myself in order to avoid conflict with someone that is being irrational and cruel towards me.

Here is the main lesson I learned; it might surprise you. It was not about John, or my health, it was actually about learning that the answers for what one needs are within oneself. Remember I shared how important it is to be present in life? Well can you imagine what might have happened to me, if I remained absent from my life, and had not done my research to figure out what was wrong with me.

Can you imagine, if I lived my entire life wondering why my father died, because I thought it was because his heart gave out because he chose cigarettes over me. I would likely be a very bitter woman right now. Instead, I learned that by doing the research, I better understood what my body was trying to tell me, and it saved my life. Then, once the doctors figured out my disorder, it just was one more piece of the puzzle that helped me reconcile that my father's death was greatly caused by the disorder we share. Of course, his health choices had something to do with it, but it would have happened even if he did not smoke. It had nothing to do with me, except that I inherited the genetic disorder. The blessing because I hated that my father smoked, and this led me to live. I have always lived a clean life with no vices.

I have a connection to my dad now that will be lifelong because this disorder does not have a cure and more importantly, my dad's death in many ways saved me. That is just how I see it. There are so many distractions in life, it can be easy to miss the little things that can alter your life forever.

Be present.

Be Intentional about it.

Really work on enhancing your awareness it could save your life, like it did mine.

CHAPTER V

ATTITUDE MATTERS

———

Remember that happy disposition I have always tried to maintain? It has saved me from a lot of hardship. I know this and I also think that I inherited some of it from my bubbly uncle Ronnie. He is my only surviving paternal uncle and he still has my dad's sense of humor. I tend to have picked up that silly dorkiness sense of humor from him. During all my surgeries, I would always tell my doctors "Hey, can you throw in a couple of boob jobs in there while you're working around the vicinity." I would say things like that just to make people laugh. I always made the doctor show me their hands and make sure they were not shaking, just always joking it off. And then realizing I am going to be in a lot of pain after each and every one of these surgeries. I was in excruciating pain, but I knew every single time the next day would always be just a bit better. If I were in the utmost pain, I'd remind myself, "The next day would be better." It was this disposition that helped me get off pain medications so quickly after my surgeries.

I have never drunk a lot or done anything to self-medicate despite the great deal of pain I have and continue to experience. I know that getting addicted to pain medication can be very easily accomplished and that it will lead you into a downward spiral. I learned this through two friends that I lost to suicide that I had tried to help. They were in similar situations of pain but turned to medication and drugs to fight their battles, and they both lost. I miss them so much.

My attitude till this day is, "It's fight mode," which for me means fight for life, fight to live, fight for strength, fight for power, fight for health. Not fight as in be a fighter or an arguer because I do not like any kind of confrontation at all. But, when I say fight mode, it

> "IT'S FIGHT MODE," WHICH FOR ME MEANS FIGHT FOR LIFE, FIGHT TO LIVE, FIGHT FOR STRENGTH, FIGHT FOR POWER, FIGHT FOR HEALTH.

means fight for survival. After surviving major surgeries, amidst chaos in my marriage, my journey started to not only survive my marriage but more importantly to survive for myself.

How did I do it?

There were five crucial steps that I have come to understand that were important to my survival.

1. Be Present.

Show up for yourself and others. In my case, my mom showed up for me when I was a teenager being bullied and during other difficult times. She was my rock and my encourager, who spoke strength into me, reminding me of all the wonderful qualities that I had and that would be realized through and in me one day. But how do you show up for yourself?

Early on that was not easy. I tried by being there for others, friends, peers, people that I thought needed me. Remember, I believed at the time that I was a peacekeeper. What I did not realize back then was that I was not showing up for myself. I felt so awkward and I was very influenced by the perceptions of everyone else about me. They said I was lanky and boyish, and I believed them. Even though I was modeling the Miami runaway, this still was not enough to block out their voices of negativity in my head. Over the years I have learned that you have to dig deep inward, in order to really appreciate what is unique about you. You have tremendous value, but if you do not recognize it for yourself, then others around you will have power and influence over you and how you see yourself.

Showing up and being present sometimes translates into being still. Not doing but rather taking the time to just be. Today I do that a lot because of my health and physical circumstances in many ways, it is demanded of me. I have to take my days one at a time. I have to stop and rest throughout the day. I take naps. My still and quiet time is spent in reflection in my garden surroundings, in order to regain physical strength for the next activity. Do not wait or allow life to serve you up a situation or condition that will demand that you do the same. Learn from me that it is especially important to be present. Fully present in your life. I have shared that I love being there for people and helping them. I believe it is part of my purpose in life. But, if I am not firstly present for myself, then I am not equipped to be of any help to anyone else.

2. Enhance your Awareness.

This lesson was learned once I found ways to regain my independence. For me, it first started with being able to get into my car that I converted with hand controls, which allowed me to be able to drive it with forearm crutches in the seat next to me. This meant not having to worry about trying to get a wheelchair into the car. This simple task is one that most people take for granted, but it meant everything to me. It meant that I could leave a situation if I needed to and to drive and go to a safe space or nowhere in particular, just away. It also meant that the limits of my physical body could be compensated by the abilities of the apparatus, in this case my car and forearm crutches. But in order to maneuver them I had to expand my field of awareness, not the typical way many able-bodied people do, but in my own unique way, based on what my abilities could and would permit. The end goal was increased independence.

It also meant finding a companion, not to do it alone. For me, the best companion in the world was and is my service dog, Chewy. Since I could now drive my two-seater sports car, Chewy could be by my side at all times. He is always right there, where I could see him. He is loyal, selfless, and so giving. My newfound ability to get back into the world, with Chewy guiding me every step, and this expanded my hope of reclaiming other aspects of my life and increased awareness of myself, others, and the world I was venturing back into.

I was getting better slowly every day. You know what supercharged my recovery even more? It was helping others after I became aware of the specific need and the unique way that I could be of service to others. Here is what I did, I got involved with the Angiomaalliance.org. Through this organization I would help people by providing them with inspiration, encouraging them to maintain upbeat thoughts and positive feelings regarding recovery in the middle of the reality of being transparent about what to expect and what they may have to go through. This outlet provided me with the opportunity to share my experiences and feelings to elevate others, and it was funny because through the process, now on the other side, others in the room would come up with things that could be planned in advance to help them after surgery. I was starting to identify a purpose of sorts, from the pain endured. Also, there was no coincidence that while I was learning to refine my attention through increased awareness, that of course there would be distractions. Things with John got even worse, if that was possible, because he started seeing me getting stronger. This in turn motivated him to start putting on the pressure more and more to bring me down under his control again. He acted quite decent in front of the family, that is during the few times that I even saw them, but behind closed doors the looming doom of what was inevitably coming was real. John still had me pretty isolated.

It is kind of funny, the more I found my strength through an identity of helping others and surviving my health challenges through increased awareness, the more I'd be afraid in my own house. Fear is a tricky emotion. It can alert you of danger, but it can also stifle you. One benefits you and the other does not.

Each day, I found myself even being scared to say the wrong thing, do the wrong thing, look at him in the wrong way or dress the wrong way. He criticized me constantly. He demanded that I regrow my hair. And God forbid I put nail polish on, I could not wear nail polish, I could not wear jewelry. Hell, no to tattoos, are you kidding me? John would have died, if he were with me today, with all the tattoos that I have now. When I was unable to grow my hair, he would call me a boy, and tell me that I looked like a boy and that he hated short hair. And I was like, I just had brain surgery, my scalp is not even attached to my skull long enough for my nerve endings to grow. This meant my hair was not growing on the one side, so it was impossible to please him. It actually took years for my hair to start growing again. You are probably thinking, how did a strong woman, who was learning so much about herself and who survived so much, find herself in the meek, bleak relationship situation still.

Well I did.

Since I was having such a difficult time growing my hair and he felt that it made me look like a boy, he started becoming fixated on his hair. John became even more vain, constantly focused on his appearance. It got so bad that if he was having a bad hair day, that was going to be a hell of a day for me. For John everything had to be perfect and if it was not, then he would be a bear. I have to admit his presentation was pristine. His hair, shoes, clothing, and closet had to be exactly right. He had everything color coordinated. But when it came to my needs or the housework that I was expected to maintain, and it had to be perfect for him. Of course, that was not physically possible for me at the time.

I swear John might have been trying to kill me, because he would leave things all over the floor knowing that I had perceptual issues and that it could take just one fall to leave me paralyzed or worse. Any time that I would trip on his things on the floor, he would say things like, "You're going to need to watch where you're going. I mean, what the F....? You have to watch where you're going." I am like, "I can't see down." He'd say, "Don't raise your voice at me." And I respond with the truth, " I can't see down, don't you understand." John knew how to get to me, to frustrate me, because he knew exactly what I was going through, but he did not care. It was all about him. As I got physically stronger, I started moving his stuff off the floor and throwing it into the closet with my crutches. Well as you might be imagining, this just set him off even more. These seemingly petty issues would lead to escalating arguments between us, the difference now was that I was getting my voice back. The increased awareness was leading to increased independence and confidence of sorts.

John was the primary financial earner at that time; and he did not let me forget it. If I started speaking out, he would remind me that I was a "tenant" in his house because he was paying all the bills. Somehow all of the first several years of our marriage, when I supported us with two and three jobs, seemed to skip his memory. It was these kinds of negative comments that ruminate in my mind from John, but I did my best to block them out and to push through with gaining independence. That involved taking drives with Chewy. This led me to learn another valuable lesson, adaptation.

3. Learn to be Adaptable

With gained independence, the open road was just me and Chewy. You might be asking why adaptability is so important. Well-read on to see my Why.

One day while driving on I-95, not too long after my surgery, about a year after, during one of those rides, I got rear-ended and I broke my neck. At the accident site they rushed me back to Mayo Clinic, I could not believe it. I just could not believe this happened. It did but there was a silver lining to this part of my story, just like in other instances, as a Duke University study patient, I became a candidate for one of the first documented bionic neck surgeries. The break was not clean, it paralyzed my arms, but I could still feel excruciating pain. The surgery was amazing. I had a metallic reconstructed neck. My MRI films were unbelievable like something out of a movie. Even today when neurologists see my films they are like, "Holy shit, that's cool." That is literally what I get from doctors all the time. When I first brought my MRI film to my neurologist, he thought it was just like the bone cadaver and the plates and bolts typically used to repair disk problems but on examination he could not believe what they had done for me. I told him, "No, no, no, it's all metal, and it wraps around my spinal cord." After I woke up from surgery I could not move my neck, but I could move my legs. It was amazing, I was fine. The pain above the area and below the area on my shoulders, and the muscular knots were real... I am still years in with therapy and occasionally I get trigger point injections and nerve blockers even now, but I can walk and have some mobility of my neck, just like you.

It was a miracle.

I was amazingly lucky enough and this was the catalyst to my affirmation that, "This is it; I'm going to get myself better, stronger. Whatever that looks like now."

I started adapting to my new reality, it was having that flexibility of mind over matter that got me moving into events working with the city and working with people, volunteering, just volunteering in my little forearm crutches and just getting out into the world. And as you might be wondering that created a lot of issues for John, because it meant I was meeting people and socializing. I was not about to remain in the misery of isolation a minute longer.

My bubbly disposition resurfaced, and I was gifted through all this hardship with a new sense. I realized that I am an 'Empath'. I learned that I could sense people's energy. I could sense good people from bad people immediately. And whenever I was around John, my whole body would just shut down. I could sense the evilness from him, so I resigned myself to surround myself with only good people. I started to develop a network of solid people and started to get a life, a new life, and a new path to follow. This led to the fourth nugget of wisdom, support.

4. Build a positive support network.

The end of my marriage, to no surprise, was initiated by John, who one day came in and gave me a letter that just stated that he had decided that he wanted to leave. He wrote that he wanted to leave and face his demons. I received it, and told myself, "Good." Here is the kicker, he wanted me to remain living in the house we shared ownership and he would pay the bills. In essence he wanted to keep me captive in his investment property. Initially I thought, there was no way I was going to do that, but then it dawned on me that I loved my house. I had designed it inside and out and my garden was my sanctuary. John, in his mind, wanted to remain married but separated because he point-blank told me that he did not want to lose his house. Remember those friends I was surrounding myself with, well they were very influential some of them, and they referred me to a great attorney. I was also seeing a therapist at the time, because I am not going lie, I was getting to my limit with my marriage and everything else I was living through, and I needed a reprieve or who knows what could have happened. This therapist helped me gain perspective and to reposition my life in a way that it gave meaning to becoming motivated to adapt and to prepare for change.

Before I could take any legal action, John would make sure that he filled my mind with all sorts of fears and threats. He once told me that if I sought a divorce, I would find myself dancing on a pole before he would give me one penny in alimony. John was even able to get one of my relatives to harass me at the time. It became a tag team effort to bully, belittle and demean me, he found in this family member a confidant, which was heartbreaking because I still was not included in family holidays and I really missed not being a part of my family. John knew that and he would use it to belittle me even more. John tried to play all kinds of mind games and I am not going to minimize the impact it had on me. There were days, minutes really, that I thought let's just end all this pain. But, then I would be reminded of what my mother had always told me, "That there is hope, that there's a new road to take. And that when one door is closing, there always will be another door opening. As long as you wake up and breathe that next morning, you have a chance. And it's how you're going to live that day and how you're going to go about doing it that matters."

It is in these moments that my now self, reminds my then self that, "You are going to be just fine and you will bloom and live a full life and have so much love in her life from friends and family and still remain hopeful maybe that special man that finally will love and cherish you (me) and if I don't that is ok too, I have always considered myself a chameleon… I just change my colors and adapt". I went through extremely low points in life, so I completely understand how someone might just want to give up sometimes, but you just cannot. It is the ***fight mode***, that is tattooed on my arm to see daily. 'You have got this' and 'fight mode', both chosen reminders I tattooed on me, so I will never forget. All you have to do is kick it into gear and surround yourself with the right support network and eliminate negativity from your life.

I did and so can you!

I got stronger. I met people. I never had to strip on a pole and I never lost my home, my castle, my sanctuary. And he had to give me more than a penny. People told me, "No, no, no, don't be silly. You'll do fine, we'll get you through this." For the first time that I could recall, I had a support system in my life. I found people that actually would take care of me besides my mother because basically, my support system was my mom my whole life. And it was so refreshing to see these people who were strangers that became close to me and held me up to give me the strength to do what I needed to do. I filed the divorce papers. And then what?

So much happened between then and now, but I want to share the fifth lesson learned, find what makes you happy.

5. Find what makes you happy.

Thus far you have learned that Chewy makes me happy. Regaining control over my own body and gaining independence made me happy. Helping others and being of service makes me happy. Also being still and quiet in my garden sanctuary that truly is my happy place. Reminders of what I know to be true from my experiences and using that knowledge to help others avoid the same mistakes I made, makes me happy. Writing this journey after all these years makes me happy. And knowing that you are reading my words makes me happy as well. Building a strong network of friends and family makes me happy, cooking, singing writing all make me happy. Just seeing a cardinal in a tree out my kitchen window makes me happy, simple joys in life, make me happy.

What makes you happy?

Ask yourself what do you love to do? Consider when you are doing it, do you feel wonderful, at peace and on purpose? If you love what you do, it never feels taxing or like a chore.

CHAPTER VI

THE SWINDLE GOES ARRAY

———⟡———

Oh, my goodness, what evil. When John gets notified of the impending divorce action, he gets so angry. He screamed and yelled at me and threatening me. It just got crazy. At the time, he was not living in the house, but I was not permitted to replace the locks on the doors until the divorce was finalized. That meant living in fear that he could come to the house whenever he wanted to harass me. I am not going to lie, I was scared. Likely more frightened than I had ever been because I just did not know what to expect from John. Often I had my mom staying at the house with me. The danger was really alright, but he had never been violent or visibly cruel towards me in front of anyone else. On the outside he was the perfect husband.

There is one other caveat to this ordeal. Remember my car accident, well I got a real nice settlement, and I had those funds in savings. I had a sense John was up to something, so I started taking copies of bank statements etc., because he started spending and spending some more. This went on for several months before he gave me his letter telling me he was moving out. He had this planned for some time and I was certain that he was going to clean out my savings from my settlement in the process of leaving. He bought cars and designer stuff, while I kept driving my same old 20-year-old car. But I was okay with it because material stuff was never that important to me, and it appeased him. I just wanted my house with my garden sanctuary and the means to pay for it and maintain it. So, I took pictures of every transaction he made. He spent tons of money.

When John got the divorce papers, he went ballistic because he did not understand the legal wording and thought that I was personally suing him. I tried to explain that a divorce is a severing of a contract, but he was not hearing it. He just went off more and it scared me. I retained an attorney with the remaining $17,000 he left in my account and I was basically left with nothing.

Although I was scared, I forged forward with my plan to retain my house and to be as fair as possible. My attorney wanted me to go after more money, but I am not that kind of person to want to do others harm in any way. I was just looking for enough to pay the house and my bills and considered my lifelong health issues. John was looking out for John, so he thought he was smart and got a low-balled appraisal on the house. My attorney got another appraisal for me and a third was presented as part of the divorce proceedings.

Recall, I had always handled all of our finances, so I knew exactly how much the house was worth and by the way, my brother is also an appraiser. When my attorney handed me the three appraisals I said, "Looks good, let's take that one [referring to John's low-ball appraisal]."

This is what happened, that appraisal was about $150,000 below what it should have been. Then after speaking with the mediator, I was able to show him the amount of money paid out to me in settlement for the broken neck I sustained in the car accident and I was able to show evidence of how much of that money had been dwindled in the last year by John's super huge spending sprees on everything he wanted. As a result, I was able to negotiate and get the house and alimony. The alimony is permanent because of my disability. As a matter of fact, the IRS considers it 'Child Support' because I am a vulnerable adult. The divorce was finalized and that is how I have financially been able to survive till now.

This was the end of an ugly chapter in my life that took up over 25 years, but it led me to realize that there was a new chapter emerging as I had found that I had a lot to offer others and something to give back to the world.

I do not want to leave you thinking that my divorce settlement set me up. Because that is not true, in fact the cost of inflation of living was not well factored in and today the amount I receive does cover my bills, but not much else. Rather, the termination of the toxic relationship in my life freed me to further my pursuit of purpose through all the pain, and to focus on the present rather than remaining stuck in my past. There was a new chapter emerging and I wanted to be present, fully aware, and adaptable. I wanted to be surrounded by positive people who were genuine, and to have the privilege to find happiness.

But…here is the reality, the desires I just shared were fueled foremost by my need to start anew. This meant staying in the moment.

I woke up one morning and realized that I am alone. I had no one else to answer to anymore, except myself. I would only need to cook for myself, and if I wanted to, I could just eat cereal. I did not care if the meal was hot enough, because everything tasted just right to me. I took amazing solace in the reality that there would be no repercussions if dinner wasn't on the table at a certain time in a certain way. It felt great! These realizations led to a series of incremental realizations, the proverbial Aw Ha moments that reaffirm to you that the decisions you have made are the right ones for you.

It was not the end of my life saga with John though, he would show up at my house uninvited, and yes, that was one of those moments when I realized, "This is my house. I have the deed of ownership and John has no right to be here." John was under the delusion that he could still come and go as he pleased to my house. On one occasion he came and started taking everything out of my garage, and I mustered my voice and told him, "I can call the police if you don't stop doing what you are doing and get off my property." Of course, this triggered his verbal belligerence and the F-bombs started spewing from his mouth like daggers, but you want to know something, they did not penetrate as deep as they had in the past. I was empowered by the reality that if I were a different kind of person, I could call the police and have John arrested. Although his words were hurtful, I was not in fear. My mom was in the house though and I knew that she was hearing all the yelling and cursing and would likely get scared, so I called her to the door. John hated my mother, so of course this escalated the situation a bit, calling my mother an old bitty… well I was used to being name called and yelled at, but was not going to accept the same treatment toward my angel of a mother… but then…this little voice from behind me, my mom, cursed back at John. Now what you have to understand is that my mom never curses, so this was so out of character for her. We both looked at each other after the words left her mouth and we started giggling a little and then shut the door!

I could not believe that my mom had cursed at John. I high fived my mom and said to her, "Let's go get a mudslide and burger to celebrate." A mudslide is what I call an adult milkshake. Just like it was rare that my mom cursed it was also just as rare to go for a mudslide, but it was a celebration, I felt liberated.

My newfound freedom in my house gave birth to a renewed passion to take care of it. There were issues with my home, several items needing fixing, but now I would be the one doing it on my own. I was not the least bit worried, in fact it empowered me to know that I was self-reliant. John had tried to drill into me that I could not survive without him over so many years of marriage. It felt so damn good that I could do things and that I continue to do them to my liking and on my own.

Do not believe the lie that you are incapable of being on your own and you can not only survive but thrive. You are equipped to survive, and skills can be learned if you don't already know them. These types of fears need to be challenged so they no longer stifle your potential.

For me, knowing that despite all of my ailments, surgeries, and ongoing medical impairments, I am perfectly capable and powerful. This gave me the confidence to know that when I would decide to open my heart again and to date, it would not be because of a need, but because I chose it, when I wanted it.

There is definitely a different level of power knowing that choices one makes are because of a want and not a need. This shifts the power differential back to the source.

The culmination of all the little but significant moments of realizations led in me to an awakening one morning of feeling like who I used to be. I was back!

My mother and others always tried to tell me that I was dying inside because John was killing every part of me that made me, who I was before him. Now I know that when people see these observable changes in a person, it's really about their essence, their soul that is being snuffed out. I honestly did feel dead inside while married to John, but now I am so grateful to the experience of my marital relationship because it resulted in an awakening.

The manifestation of my awakening took the form of self-expression. While married I did not wear what I wanted, grow my hair, or even put on make-up too often. I did not even paint my nails with polish, for fear of criticism. Can you imagine there were no positive affirmations that I was pretty, attractive, rather everything that came out of John's mouth was derogatory and meant to tear me down. So now I started growing out my hair.

It became this beauty long mane, curly, not always perfect, but totally reflective of my spirit. I explored my tastes in clothing, make-up options and nail polish. It may seem like little things for some, but in the context of my life, it was significant. I mixed colors and totally let my creative side come out. And behold what I love most about myself began to shine again. Even the scares. The reminders of all of my past surgeries became my landscape to express my creative.

The creative flow manifested through one tattoo to tell the story of life and today my life story is written through images that cover not only physical but the emotional scars of my past. Along my entire back I have the image of a beautiful cherry blossoms and a nest with a swallow tail bird, which means, "New life. New beginnings." Each and every tattoo has a bit of my story. I have one that is the real handwritten note my mom gave me for one of my birthdays and it has her signature and the words "Love you, mommy." On my left arm along with Mom's love note, I have a tattoo of my Dad's favorite flower stem and a rose along the main artery of my heart. On the same arm I also have the honeybee and flowers my current boyfriend gave me, along with a musical note all representing my gifting in music that my boyfriend helped me realize. I have always loved to sing, but until him, I had not ever thought to do it. Honeybee is the name of our musical group. I have every furry friend I've had in my life somewhere tattooed on my body, but the most meaningful is my tattoo under my right wrist of Chewy's paw print. Chewy has been through so much with me, always by my side, supporting me emotionally, when it was so needed. Chewy is nearing retirement, but no matter what, he will always be my right-hand man and his tattoo will be with me forever. These tattoos are a passage, a show of strength, visuals of a life well lived, yes there has been pain and suffering, but also beauty beyond measure.

The ashes that rose from my pain were many, but of them I have found passion and purpose in my creative with music, art and in serving people and my furry babies.

What passion has risen from a difficult situation for you?

Reflect, is there anything that I am totally in love with doing now? Be in the moment when you are thinking about it. What do you feel? If thinking about it alone lights you up, then jot it down here as this is a clue into your passion-points.

CHAPTER VII

THE BEACON

Shortly after my divorce, whilst I was still volunteering, I was able to rekindle a love of Meteorology. I am a university graduate of the discipline; this is just another aspect of myself that was derailed due to health issues during my draining marriage. While interning at a local weather station, I suffered a stroke. This disruption was difficult to return from, but what made it almost impossible was the lack of support from John. When there are people close to you that you give the power of influencing you and they are intent on belittling you, be on guard. It is a significant sign when others have to put you down in order to help themselves feel some kind of way. John had me believing that I was not good at anything, including my trained profession. He would go as far as to tell me, what would any of these intelligent women have in common with you, just to increase that self-doubt that I was not good enough, for a moment it worked as I do have some brain damage from my brain surgery and I do get stuck on words and such. But I was far from stupid and I quickly learned i was and always had been so called good enough and his comments stemmed from his own low self-worth that was projected on me.

Early into our marriage, I was seeking employment in my profession and I landed a great weather anchor job offer, but because of the incremental negative internal dialogue that kept resounding John's negative words to me, and the set back from numerous strokes, I gave it up before I even realized where it could have led me in my career. This time though, I was not going to allow anything to derail me, I started my own weather page on Facebook called Florida Severe Weather. Initially it was to help people online, friends, family, and fishermen, navigate the weather patterns. Back then I had a small following.

To start small is perfectly okay, that is actually the best place for anyone, as it allows for the development of confidence through experience. Initially my weather channel did not immediately take off, and the fact that I took on a partner, a businessman, who ironically had also started a similar weather page, did not help. After spending tens of thousands of hours and resources, I quickly came to realize i was running this page on my own. I persevered despite the limited outcomes, and over time became trusted by my audience, due to my accurate hurricane warnings and such. It felt so good, helping people, but also the fact that the little negative voice in my head was being snuffed out, silenced and I was again realizing a life dream to be a meteorologist.

Don't ever give up on your dreams.

Not so long afterward, that business partner went ghost on me for months, but it did not phase me as it might before. Instead it fueled me to continue on with the work and before I knew it I was being recognized by FEMA and NOAA for my meteorology work. If you are not familiar with these organizations, they are the holy grail, the best practice in my field. The organizations invited me to their respective headquarters to visit the hurricane hunting planes, it was a wonderful time in my career. Then that partner, I mentioned resurfaced, but now he wanted to engage in a formal contractual arrangement with me and something inside told me it was not in my best interest.

Listen to your intuition, it is based on past experience.

I did just that and sought counsel and sure enough, I was encouraged to go on at it alone. The prospective business partner did not appreciate my empowerment and tried to block me and to discredit me in the community, but those who knew me realized his scam, and this led me to entrepreneurship, as I created my own page again.

You might be thinking wow all that work and then to have to start over. I agree with your sentiment, but hindsight is twenty-twenty, had I remained in that toxic business relationship who knows where it would have led. Instead I decided it was best to go it alone.

Over the last eight years, my weather page has grown into the triple digits of followers. I love the work and I have an engaged audience, who trust and respect the work I do. Sure, it is all volunteer and altruistic, but it feeds my soul in a way that is priceless.

Do you want to know the key to how I did it?

I activated my trusty fight mode, by leaning into the creative affirmations and visual on my body and empowered myself to realize that I was capable. Sometimes even when you are engaged in your passion work, you may come across, not rather, you will undoubtedly come across adversities and challenges. Remember failures are just experiences to learn from but do not allow them to create blocks.

I felt honored by each person that followed me on my FB page and they knew that I was committed to the work with authenticity and transparency. What they did not see was that sometimes I needed a cry day, just to process the feelings, and that is okay. Give yourself a cry day every so often if you need it. Then brush yourself off and face the world again. Every time that I am knocked down, I see the potential for embitterment and have to refocus on my path. There is a caveat here though, you have to know your purpose in doing what you love. For me it is the desire to want to help others. As a young child I always saved injured and stray animals even volunteered as a teenager at an injured duck sanctuary. This led to an outgrowth of empathy and love which are great gifts that need to be embraced unconditionally in life, no matter what. I took on these activities in the midst of experiencing tremendous bullying in school, and building empathy and compassion actually gave me a different perspective on the bullying experience. I became curious about what could be going on with the bullies that they had to behave this way towards me, instead of just hating them for what they were doing to me.

When I was 16, I will never forget when I met a homeless man that everyone seemed to ignore. A group of teenaged boys were beating on him and I was the only one who ran towards the homeless man, yelling at the boys to stop it! Luckily, the boys ran away, because I really had not stopped to think about what I was doing and the possible consequences to my own safety. Rather in instinct I just ran towards the danger. A nearby hotel manager saw and called for an ambulance, while I remained with the homeless man, who was unconscious. I had his bloody head cradled in my arms and his head, eyes, and lips, as well as arms were all swelling up. I never saw that man again and I never did get any details about him afterwards. I just knew that he needed help. No matter what negative experience you are going through, do not allow it to rob you of your compassion and love for others. If you can nurture these then even negative experiences have purpose.

I am often doing acts of random kindness to further develop my empathy and compassion for others. Particularly, if I find myself in a challenging situation, like after one of my surgeries and a family tiff, I ended up on Thanksgiving in a restaurant. I looked over and there was a police officer all alone. I shifted my mind away from my own troubles and I focused on what I could do. I ended up paying for the police officer's meal and this made me feel great. It was one of the most memorable Thanksgiving memories that I have.

On another occasion, during mine and my girlfriends typical Tuesday outings, it was one of those rare freeze-over days in Florida, but we went out anyways. For me it was novel, because cold weather in South Florida is not common, but my girlfriend was from Philly, so she was not liking the weather at all. We went to our customary community hangout joint, and saw the same homeless man, who never spoke to anyone, outside appearing very cold. While we were there enjoying our time, I bought the man a coffee and for the first time he smiled at me. Before we left for the evening, I gave the joint owner a twenty and asked him to feed and to continue giving the man coffee, while he remained on their property. I knew that they would honor my request and later I learned that they did. That evening I was the warmest I had ever felt, in below freezing weather.

Another one of my identified passions is volunteering and inspiring others who find themselves in similar situations to where I have been in the past. I still volunteer at the Brain and Spinal Cord Institute for women. Through my work there, I remind people that science has limits and that even when you are told you will not walk again, or that you have reached maximum medical benefit, I call "bull crap" because I'm living proof that if you go into *fight mode*, you can push limits. I know that I have permanent disabilities, but I prefer to focus on my abilities instead.

I KNOW THAT I HAVE PERMANENT DISABILITIES, BUT I PREFER TO FOCUS ON MY ABILITIES INSTEAD.

Remember the importance of being adaptable, you need to find the new rhythm of life sometimes, and that is okay.

Your life may have to be modified. I take breaks, naps even during the day. But I am very productive. In addition to volunteering at the institute, I also now mentor women in domestic violence situations. From everything that I learned from first-hand experience, I share what they too might be going through, so that they can see light, where sometimes it seems that there is only darkness, and no one understands. I remind them of their worth, that they are not crazy and that others can be cruel and very manipulative to keep control over them. I remind them the sky will shine again and that they have to trust their instincts, their inner voice. That they have to trust their intuition. This work is rewarding.

I love animals, almost as much as I do people. So of course, I volunteer at the zoo with my service dog, I just love to give back to society. I often visit hospitals and visit stroke patients and elderly people with my service dog. I love to bring smiles to everybody since I remember what it felt like when I was in the hospital and having a doggy day on Wednesday would make my day. Chewy is such an amazing companion who also enjoys these outings.

No matter what is going on in your life, just remember to be grateful. There is so much to be happy about, especially the little things in life that people just do not open their eyes and see anymore. I would see them even at my darkest times like right when the pain got unbearable. Like even right now, I see the best little things in this sharing process of writing.

Right now, I am in bed, I have all of my kitty cats and dogs sitting right next to me. They are embracing me; they are supporting me, and I am so grateful to have them here with me. There is always something to be happy or grateful about. When you become aware, then you gain enlightenment and an inner peace that serves to center you, so that you can focus on your strength in that particular moment.

Join me in an exercise of awareness.

I would like you to get into a comfortable seated position. To square your hips and loosely allow your arms to drop on either side of your body. Center your mind on whatever thoughts are flowing through your consciousness. Now breathe. Be aware of each breath, as you inhale and exhale. Take a few breaths to center and align. Now that you are relaxed, I want you to activate your senses, take in whatever the world is wanting you to see, hear, smell, taste and feel. Stay still for a few minutes. For as long as it feels comfortable.

Now reflect on what you learned from your senses. Jot down a few thoughts about what you saw, heard, smelled, or tasted, as well as how it all made you feel. We need to practice remaining in the moment, to gain increased awareness and to cultivate gratitude.

_____

_____

_____

_____

_____

_____

_____

_____

_____

CHAPTER VIII

THE BUTTERFLY PHASE

———✦———

The butterfly phase…is my truth because I felt entrapped in a cocoon for most of my life. My mind and my heart and even my body at times betrayed me and were paralyzed for periods. But once I hit 42 years of age, I entered the second phase of my life. During this phase, I experienced amazing surrender and release from the cocoon, and I became a new butterfly ready to soar.

During my time to transform, I had not realized how the world had changed. Boy did I have a lot to learn. I had to learn how to do simple things like change a hi-hat light bulb, do the outside landscaping lights and other odds and ends to fix up my house just as I wanted it. My home was and is my sanctuary. My need to be self-sufficient was fueled by the memories of those times that I had been ridiculed for my housework throughout my marriage. Now there was no one to ridicule and say that I was doing things incorrectly. In the second phase of my life, it was all about how I wanted to do it and you know what it was always done right. I felt in my heart and soul that the release of pressure and tension and my newfound faith in myself meant that things were being done right.

Even the gardening, which was the only thing that John really did as a husband, was now just how I wanted it, beautiful and without pesticides. I had always begged him to stop putting chemicals and poison on everything in the garden but monthly he would put so much spray and poisons to kill every little bug and all the caterpillars, so we never saw a butterfly. We never had birds, he killed several fish in my koi pond and still he would not heed me that it was because of the sprays and chemicals that he was using.

Right now, in this present moment my garden is pest-control free, absolutely gorgeous, yes, I have lost a couple of plants here and there due to infestations, but I do have tons of butterflies, dragonflies, birds and beautiful caterpillars waiting to also spread their wings and fly.

Now each new morning is met with my smile, because I am awake and alive. The last part I don't take for granted, because on multiple occasions in my past my health issues had made my survival tenuous. I am grateful and very thankful for the new day itself. Each new day is started with a sense of peace and tranquility and all my animals and pets are calm and happy because I am calm and happy. This overwhelming sense of peace transcends to freedom, and with faith in yourself and being centered to know that what you do is enough, what you do is right...as long as it is in your heart and soul, is priceless. Being right is not so important, but following your intuition is. Certainly, do not allow the fear of someone else's constant criticism and bullying put you down or prevent you from living, fully living.

Wake up every morning with a smile, like I do. The first face I typically see is of my service dog who is my right-hand man. He is always there for me, and he does such an amazing job keeping me safe, with joy. I also see all the cats welcoming me and I no longer have the stress overwhelming me to immediately do my chores.

My fish are thriving and actually I am on my fifth generation of spawns. The man who cleans the fishpond says he's never seen that before in captivity and I tell him that it is because they are happy fish living in a sanctuary that I made sure to provide for them poison free, stress-free and with all my love.

My home and environment were and are just as I always dreamed it.

Since now my home was in order, I turned to redefining my newfound freedom in a new world. I continued to expand my social circle, making some friends and I was very proud of myself for getting out into the world, even though I had such fear and anxiety that overwhelmed me at times it was just those baby steps to get out of the house. I had my vehicle converted to have hand controls, and this also increased my independence to run errands and to get out and about. Whenever I was approached by anyone in the community, Chewy was so helpful in getting me to open up and talk to people, as over the years I had become shy and uncomfortable talking. I had a lingering fear towards men that influenced me and how I related with the opposite sex. That is until I addressed it. Afterwards, I became confident that I was ready to explore the world, especially the dating world.

We were not created to live in a vacuum alone, but in community. Do not shy away from this truth.

If anyone ever tries to shame you for seeking help, please eliminate that person from your trusted inner circle. They do not have your best interest at heart. Getting the help, you need is courageous and takes strength. It is in no way an indication of weakness of any kind. I did, and once I did, I learned so much about what I had actually experienced in my marriage to a person with a narcissistic personality. Getting the help that I needed equipped me with strategies in my toolkit to move forward even in my interpersonal life. Ultimately it helped me gain a new perspective on myself, others and the way people can interact with one another.

Spread Your Wings

I was ready to feel those romantic aspirations again. It was time, I started going out with one of the girls that I met at a political campaign and she and I would go out to the clubs to dance and drink. I never did drugs or anything like that, but I did start drinking more than I likely should have. But, if I am honest, those early days of freedom, I did let loose and I thought

I deserved it. This was my time to spread my wings and fly and see what the world was like.

I met several more girlfriends and we would be out all the time dancing, drinking, going to my local pubs and several other places for happy hour. During this time, a few girlfriends that did not do the party scene because they were married, took me into their circle. I became close with one, because she had never really seen the world all that much and I would take her to nature parks and the beach. We would witness the moonrise at the beach at night. Things I loved to do, but they were now so much nicer doing them with a friend. Her and I got close …her family is my family. Her daughter became like a daughter to me. This girlfriend and her family led me back to a part of my life that I was missing, the sense of belonging to a family again. We would have family fun nights or family fun days that were just filled with joy and laughter. This was something I had not had in a long time with my own family and never with my ex-husband. It was after developing this familial relationship that I pulled away from the bars and the party scene. It was a great time in my life, but I was beginning to feel a bit lonely and started thinking about looking for a partner to enjoy life with.

But please remember, do not stay in an unhealthy relationship in fear of being alone, because I was more alone in a loveless marriage, than I was now fulfilled with love from friends that surrounded me.

Facebook was a big thing about 10 years ago, and I was introduced to it as a means to just connect and to follow bands that I liked. At least that is how I used it. My girlfriends and I really liked certain bands and we would follow them on FB to know where they were playing and to get tickets for their concerts. Some of the band pages had chat rooms and you could engage with the musicians and their fans. It was all so novel for me as I had been sheltered, isolated from all of this while married.

One of the first men I dated I met at my local pub, not on a going out party day but during one of our music events that was held there for a protest that was to support Non-GMOs in our food. I met a great network of people that were involved in events for this cause and a man, Rick.

I became immediately smitten with Rick. He was very handsome with really nice blue eyes and he just seemed like a gentle soul and generous. He bought everyone at our table a drink and by the end of the night he asked for my number. Talk about naïve. I regressed back to that teenage girl, in an adult body, who became almost instantly infatuated.

For a couple of our dates he was nice, and I was a good girl, I did not sleep with him right away. But I quickly started falling deeper and deeper into him and the one thing that my husband never did was kiss me and boy could this man kiss. He had it down to a science. He was very gentle, slow, not a lot of tongue, just so sweet and loving. He had me convinced he was a good guy. Even with all the lessons learned, I am not going to sugar coat things, I remained somewhat naïve about men. This was my one area of lingering vulnerability: a blind spot.

I definitely was clear about my desire to want to remain independent, but I was so drawn to him. I was just not able to do anything; I was like a lovestruck kid. I could not think straight and felt butterflies and everything like that; and thought wow he is the one. The only red flag that I initially identified was that we would go out a couple of weeks in a row and things were awesome, great even. But then I would not hear from him. I would try texting him and calling him. One time he stood me up. I got all dressed up, and waited, and waited and he never showed up. Then the phone rang, and it was him telling me how much he missed me and how sorry he was that he let me down.

Red flat alert - Ghosting

I found myself in a familiar place, in a relationship where I was doing everything to please Rick, but he was never there for me only when he felt like it and then it was every now and then. I knew I was being abused with ghosting techniques but still I stayed invested in the relationship. I now see how the experience was another learning opportunity for me. The funny part was that even thought I knew what was going on, every so often when Rick would call, I would find myself forgiving him and wanting to spend time with him. I just still had not gained the strength to tell him to go to hell. I think it's because I wanted the relationship to work out, and I found myself in a cycle that I knew was going nowhere. Enter Jose, to rescue me.

Red Flag alert, love bombing.

While trying to get over Rick. I briefly met a member of the U2byUV band, but it didn't last. While out one night watching the band though I met another interesting man, Jose. Jose ended up finding me on the U2byUV webpage and reached out. What he didn't know at the time was that he was meeting a girl with a broken heart, who was emotionally unavailable. Jose was also going through his own drama, a divorce. He shared all this personal information and affirmed that since we were both in not the best of situations, we would just be friends.

Throughout our supposed 'friendship' Jose only talked about his divorce, his ex, and how they had tried different ways to end their relationship amicably. It took a long time to figure out that he was just playing with my sentiment. Especially since he played the friendship card so well. He truly became a best friend and confidant.

Concurrently, I continued being sociable. I was going out with girlfriends regularly; my social calendar was full. I loved and had the opportunity to hear and follow bands I loved, which fueled my soul, but the entire time thinking to myself, "This guy [Jose] is going through so much and he is such a good friend..."

As my friendship with Jose continued to blossom, Rick would periodically come back into my life. I wish I could share that I was strong enough to keep him out, but I wasn't. Rick always told me what I wanted to hear. Such as how beautiful, amazing, and kick-ass I was. Be careful ladies, love bombing plays into the state of your Ego. Therefore, check it to ensure that you do not need these affirmations from the outside to know your worth.

I never saw Rick during holidays, and I started to get even more suspicious because he would drink, sometimes to excess, and I would be the one to be the designated driver and everything. I was getting pretty tired of the routine with Rick, but it was as if he knew what I was thinking, because just as I was going to…he would Love-Bomb me yet again. He would tell me that he loved me so much and that he could not be without me and this talk would suck me right back into the relationship with him.

Jose, he stuck around through all of this and he repeatedly tried to be the knight in shining armor, swooping in to save me whenever Rick would let me down. Rick was an educated man, successful, a CEO. I repeatedly made excuses for his behavior and his drinking. Until one day while I was at his place, I went to go get a drink and grabbed a Gatorade bottle and started chugging it down, before I realized that it was pure vodka. I almost choked,

I thought, "What the hell." I checked the rest of the Gatorade bottles in his refrigerator and they too were all filled with vodka and then it clicked, and I knew, and everything started to make sense. Why he would leave the house so early and supposedly go to his bed, but it was to go and drink. This is why he would go dark for a while on me and not communicate with me, because he would go on drinking binges or into rehab for some period of time. Rick even moved away for a while, and during this time, he repeatedly asked me to marry him. But my intuition told me something was off, so I never conceded to marriage, I knew he just wanted to keep the fishing line baited and hooked in my mouth and he would pull on the fishing line whenever he wanted. I knew I was being toyed with and this was not ok. I knew that I wanted a partner in life that would love me as much as I loved them and that we would take care of one another. I thought Rick was that man for me at the time, but the tells were so evident.

Meanwhile my friend José, who had been in the backdrop all the while, remained steadfast in my life. About eight months into our 'friendship', I realized that he had in fact been courting me. It was not familiar to me, because it was in a way I had never been treated before, like a queen. But things between us started to change. Remember he had been my confidant throughout my relationship with Rick, my rock, who listened to me as an amazing friend would, without judgement and always so compassionate and caring. Jose was still going through it with his divorce, so our relationship had remained platonic, until that night on the restaurant rooftop. The intimate encounter changed everything.

Jose was a best friend. I thought how perfect it was to feel this loved by a best friend. I felt so comfortable with him. I told him everything and I would come to realize that I had divulged way too much to him. As our relationship grew, we would travel together, we did everything together. Yet, I would come to learn that he had a whole separate life apart from me. Jose was not seeking a divorce at all, he remained married and totally actively married with his wife.

I found myself in totally unchartered water, in an amazing love affair that started with everything I thought I wanted. He bettered himself while we were together, and we were contemplating even starting a business together. He had me believing we would be holding hands and living together into our eighties sitting on a bench. Jose was very attentive. He constantly would send text messages, love bombing me. This relationship went on for years before I was any wiser. He had me totally convinced he was a single man, unencumbered. He even moved into my home with me. This was the turning point of the deception because I am a light sleeper and my house is one-story, making it difficult for him to sneak out to his other life.

There were several times I had doubts about his honesty but boy he was good he could stare right into my eyes and just tell me so many things. Things anyone would want to hear. He was so good at that, I knew all his friends, and this was his safety net to lure me in even further, because it gave me a false sense of security. Instead of isolating me, he was showing me off to his friends.

During the holidays Jose would always say, "Well Bella I have to see my kids." There were times that I wondered why it was that he had not introduced me to his kids, because he knew that I loved kids. The reality was that Jose knew so much intimate stuff about me and my past that he knew exactly how to manipulate every situation to keep me off balance literally. He knew he had a good sucker in me because he knew my dad and mom's history of living separate lives, in separate rooms. Yeah that's right, I suspect my father had another family also. I once found a picture of a woman with a child in his wallet, who looked just like my father. It was never confirmed but it explained why my parents were not affectionate with one another during my childhood. Also, why it was that they lived separate lives albeit in the same household, just to give me a family upbringing with both of my parents under the same roof.

Jose and I ended up sleeping in separate rooms at one point in our relationship nearing the end. But it all seemed all too familiar to my experience as a child with my own parents. My parents loved one another, in their own way. Just like I had fallen in love with Jose, so why would I suspect anything was wrong.

My mom met Jose and she tried to warn me, saying that he was like a character in a perfect fairytale, too good to be true. I know that she knew his truth, and she tried to save me the heartache, but I had to go through the experience for its own value.

Periodically Rick would still reach out to me, I often thought, "What a fool he was if only...". Rick never admitted he had a drinking problem. I always thought if he would just admit that he was an alcoholic and be willing to get help, I am the type of person who would have been right by his side in support. Of course, that never happened. As charming as Rick was it was almost time to let him go for good and especially after the last time I saw him walking out of an AA meeting and I told him, "I'm so proud of you, I'm very happy to see that you're going to an AA meeting," and his response was, "I wasn't at an AA meeting what are you talking about." I knew then that he was still hiding his problem and not ready to accept help. So, I let him go.

I so hope that he has done okay in life.

Jose and I had a lot of fun doing things I had never experienced before with a man. I guess that is just it, Jose was a good friend, therefore going out to concerts, having picnics, and just having fun, was all part of our dynamic. So strikingly different from Rick or John. Jose was very affectionate and when he was with me, it was all about me. I was the center of his universe and for a time, it felt so good.

I had reconnected with myself after my divorce from John. I knew who I was but the newness of who I was becoming was all intriguing. Unlike Jose, John never looked at me in the eyes, or kissed me. Many people in my life at the time of my marriage questioned John's masculinity, as most people thought he might be struggling with being gay and just not out of the closet. Our marriage might have just been his front, an experiment, I am not certain, but I do know that he was a great deal vainer and more self-absorbed in his looks and whatnot, than I ever was. He could not walk by a mirror without checking himself out and he used to watch very questionable movies about gay lifestyle. Maybe that was it, he was frustrated in a marriage with a woman. It was not me at all.

Red flag alert, grandiosity. It is only a cover for their weak insecure ego.

Jose was different, he saw all of my femininity and he celebrated it all the time, making me feel more of a woman than I had in the past. It must be cultural; they say Latin men are the true quintessential lovers. Their masculinity is part of their being, and as an alpha male, they easily empower our femininity.

Confusing right, I know that is why I am sharing my experiences so transparently. I want to save even one other person from going through all that I did while dating in the second phase of life.

I remember one time getting bit by a black Asian Wasp on an outing with Jose. These types of bites are the most excruciating one can possibly experience other than a scorpion, according to the hospital emergency staff. This happened to me when Jose was all consumed with taking me to the rocket launching. After I got bit, I wanted to be taken to the hospital, but Jose became all irritated. I now became an inconvenience, and he began reiterating that he did not drive all this way to take me to the hospital. He told me to put ice on it, and to watch the launch. I did of course, and by mid-early morning the next day I was having convulsions because I developed a 102° temperature. I had to be rushed to the hospital, but when we got there, even though I was apparently in a serious state, Jose was watching girl skateboarding videos and acting angry with me for getting hurt. I thought to myself, "This totally reminds me of John when I was bitten by a raccoon and I had to get 68 rounds of rabies shots.

John saw me in excruciating pain, and he did not even hold my hand. The doctor had to actually yell at John telling him to at least "Hold her feet do something." I saw Jose's mask slightly fall off that day because I saw a glimpse of the monster my ex-husband had been towards me on so many similar occasions when I was injured.

I am forgiving.

There is a part of me that will always give others the benefit of the doubt. It was this belief that led me to allow Jose back into my life, even after I disclosed his infidelity to his wife.

Jose and his pro-golfing buddies were all in a pack to be married, and to have sweet unsuspecting blond girlfriends on the side. It was part of the culture Jose was a part. None of the wives or girlfriends for that matter knew what was going on, but once I found out, I made sure that at least Jose's wife knew. A lot of chaos occurred as a result, but what is important to share here is that Jose eventually circled back to me, begging to reconcile, swearing that he had gotten the divorce and even showing me the decree. I believed him because after all he had been my most trusted best friend.

The second round of deception did not last too long, before both his wife and I realized that he was up to his old antics again. Afterwards, Jose's wife and I became acquaintances, we compared notes about experiences we had thought were unique to ourselves, only to find out that Jose had duplicated almost exactly everything he said and did with one of us with the other. It was all disgusting.

This relationship was difficult to reconcile not because I could not believe it could happen, but because we were such close friends and confidants before we were ever romantically involved. I do not know what happened to Jose, but I do know that his wife was totally informed. Neither of us were in the dark.

Red flat alert – distortion of the truth for self-gain

Life is about learning. The few years after my divorce allowed me to experience heart lessons that taught me that I still had learning to do in my forties. The most important lesson was a need to focus on learning to love myself. I decided to take a year off from dating and meeting men. I wanted time to heal and to reclaim myself.

During that time, I enjoyed my life by going to the beach, into nature, being with my animals, my family, especially my mom, and cultivated my relationships with my girlfriends. We did all sorts of fun things like silly family game nights with my friends' family members, boating and fishing as I love the outdoors.

The time alone gave bloom to further affirmation of my self-worth. I realized that I have a lot to offer. I was perfectly fine with who I was and happy with my life. I really learned how to stay focused and centered and realized that I am good alone. I am wonderful alone, and my time alone elongated my wingspan to soar even higher.

There are times when it may appear as though darkness can snuff out light but that is not possible, Light is a beacon. There will be storms but continue to shine your beacon brighter. Do not allow the darkness to roll-in to the point that it is overpowering. In my life, it took the form of increased service to others, to counterbalance the losses from personal interactions through dating.

I focused on spreading love, smiling at strangers, opening doors for women and men alike, and if there was no acknowledgement or thank you then I remind myself that, "It's okay, you do exist and you're doing the right thing just keep doing it no matter what."

No matter what occurs in life, keep on shining the light.

Always smile.

Always help others.

That is basically how I continue to live my life.

Despite the momentary pause during which dating took a back seat for a while, I experienced my most valuable love story with myself. The process might sound lonely, but in fact the truth is that we are never alone. My life was filled with beautiful friends, my mom and brother and my many furry friends who surrounded me with unconditional love. It was all life affirming. That does not mean that you close yourself off to love, but in my case it had to occur organically as I was no longer looking for it, at least not actively in a romantic manner. The key though is to keep yourself open to the possibility of finding love.

Here is a takeaway from my dating experiences: do not compromise. Develop non-negotiables. I decided right then that whoever could be my someone someday would need to fit into alignment with the life that I had created for myself. The connection between souls had to feel comfortable and natural, building upon real sustainable love.

As the year passed the focus remained on enjoying life in every aspect of it. The awakening of awareness was sweet, as it provided opportunities to pause and take in those otherwise overlooked moments in life. I had never enjoyed family time holidays with my girlfriend and her family as much, and with my own family, mom, and brothers. I'm not going to tell you that I didn't wish that my other relatives and close family ties improved, because they really didn't, but I accepted it, and remained present and in gratitude for every moment with those special people and furry friends in my life.

During my dating hiatus I took to running my weather page, it was passionately creative, and I enjoyed it tremendously. However, it was also a conduit for men to feel inclined to connect with me and to attempt to court me via my media channels. I would talk to each of them and be cordial, but then before leading them towards something I was not looking for, I would clarify that I was not interested or actively dating at the time. There was the occasional creep that made me extremely glad that I was out of the dating scene for a while. One thing though, my tolerance for pests and undesirables was very keen and I would immediately identify those men and cut them off. In return they would tell me niceties such as you're going to grow old alone. I would think to myself, "Well there ya go Linda you just weeded out that jerk…I'd rather be alone than to be with someone that felt he would be the only thing I needed to fulfill my life." A few of the men I met online were truly kind and respectful and I would find myself helping them with girl issues and just being a friend. I enjoyed being a support and counsel of sorts, and I felt that I was a good listener. But the minute I sensed that the person was toeing the line of a romantic pursuit, I would kindly reiterate that I was not dating at the moment . I was lucky because part of my page rules is that folks know that respect was of utmost importance and that my site was not a dating site. This disclaimer weeded out many people.

Over time, I got to know a few people well through my weather page, and one stuck out. He had nice eyes and a nice smile, but I was concerned because he was in a band and I had already dated the musician type before. He was persevering though because he engaged in online communication with me for almost eight months before he convinced me to meet him offline for lunch. Actually, I made it clear that it was not a date, but rather a business meeting. I knew he was phishing, and I needed to be careful. I reminded myself to use all those past lessons learned to avoid pain from romantic heartbreak.

Yes, I went to the lunch, but guarded. We met at the agreed-on location and chatted and drank water over a 5-hour meeting. I found he was quite easy to talk to and seemed like a nice guy. He later told me that he had never met someone with whom he had sat and drank water only and talked five hours straight. It was nice. No pressure. It took a little time, but we did eventually go on a real date and it too went well. Then I found myself showing him around my neighborhood and he shared the same with me. It has now been almost two years since we first met, and although it has not all been a fairytale, the difference in our relationship is that I speak up for myself and I listen to my intuition. I also have non-negotiables; like I will not allow anyone to disrespect me or my boundaries.

The past relationship experiences in life made me wiser. I see that now. It is sometimes difficult to have 20/20 vision in the moment unless you learn to intentionally activate your lens informed by your past experience learning.

A few other red flags identified from my experience of toxic relationships to look out for are:

i) Love bombing,

ii) Subtle digs that erode your self-esteem and worth,

iii) Grandiosity

iv) Faking it till you make it

v) Mother issues

vi) Truth distortions,

vii) Blaming and shaming,

viii) Negative gossip about all former partners,

viv) Disrespect of boundaries.

That memorable first date with Dave started with the planting of a seed of trust, that I am committed to. However, each relationship has and will have its trials, but when there is acceptance, unconditional love, and commitment most storms can be weathered. However, i made clear on the first date that trust, loyalty, friendship, and the ability to communicate without being defensive or judgmental are extremely important to me. Life will always throw curveballs, just stick to what is important to you.

The first year of my relationship with Dave was challenged by these life inconveniences, but it allowed him to witness my ability to activate my fight mode to persevere through it all like a Warrior. My mindset never wavered from positivity and a focus on the good amidst it all.

Now 50, there was another cool experience that resulted from all my personal growth, I had a big birthday party and I decided to invite my sister. The party was a complete success because I was able to just hang out and laugh with my sister after so many years of estrangement. This was possible because I let the past lay quiet in my heart and just enjoyed the moment. We danced and drank and celebrated with all my friends and family at my favorite pub listening to my friend's band...it was a great night! Best of all was that I danced with my sister and that she whispered in my ear that she had missed me. This single intersecting incident in our lives revived our relationship. I regained my sister, but the rest of the family, particularly my sister-in-law was not okay with our reconciliation and she started her old antics. My brother's wife, if you recall, was one of the mean girls in school, who just never changed her ways. She has always been the wedge between me and members of the family.

Once a bully always a bully.

Despite others' meddling, my sister is still in my life. We enjoy family holidays together again. The best gift of all is that my mom is really happy with our reconciliation. I've been able to reconnect with my niece and we are close-knit again. My niece has grown to be an amazing beautiful talented young lady. My sister did a great job raising her. I also have had the opportunity to meet and to get to know my estranged nephew. I missed so many of his early years growing up because of our estrangement, but I don't focus on the loss, rather I am grateful for the new-found love and opportunity.

My family was reconciling and reunited again, and this made me incredibly happy, but triggered my sister-in-law of course. Shortly thereafter her manipulations started up again, but this time, her antics were extinguished by our united front. My family is not perfect, but we are far from messed up. In fact, I believe my family is awesome and beautiful, not different than most families, with its chaos at times. The principal instigator of conflicts between us has been my brother's wife [the bully] for as long as I can remember. But this time we all saw through her masquerade and she was shut down.

As I am typing the last few words of my story to share with you, my beacon shines bright and continuous despite the storms in life that are unavoidable. My light remains fueled by an unwavering positive attitude, gratitude, lessons learned, and the support of those who truly love me.

Currently I have water in my lungs and around my heart and an enlarged thyroid. We are in the middle of a global pandemic, and I've had to be taken to the hospital with shortness of breath and chest pain radiating into my throat and down my arm repeatedly. The most recent tests revealed that I contracted COVID-19. The deadly virus that has claimed the life of over 200,000 Americans in six months. Although I've survived the initial diagnosis, now I'm contending with the residual aftermath the virus reaps on one's organs.

During one of my recent hospitalizations, I was laying in the hospital bed and the nurses and doctors saw my tattoo that says, "I Got This" and they said, "You got this?" I then showed them my other tattoo that says, "FIGHT MODE" and told them as I rise and smiled and said "We only use 10 percent of our brains, I always tap into that other 90 percent...watch me", after all I have so much to live for even in a world with a rare pandemic and struggling to breathe. I am grateful for my united family, my furry babies, my garden and most importantly wonderful, caring network of friends and family caring for each other, thru all of this and remember to appreciate everything you do have." Don't ever forget that love is not something you have to go find, it will always be within you, so respect and love yourself first, then everything else will fall into its proper place. Look for those red flags to help you navigate the stormy seas. Life will be back to normal one day, maybe my band 'Honeybee' will be out and about once again, singing our Healthy hearts out. I knew I loved to write music and sing, I was encouraged to break through my fear and build my confidence, I never knew how much I loved to sing live and entertain. It is so gratifying to find your niche even at 50 years young and you find special people in your life to embrace it with you. We all lift each other up and soar together. So yes, as I smile at the doctors and nurses in these uncharted stormy seas, my beacon is shining bright and I sure hope I helped you to shine yours bright as well.

ABOUT THE AUTHOR

---

*L*inda Somers has learned how to look at the bright side of things, always looking for the little signs to help Her follow her untended path in life, loyal friend, daughter, sister. She is a huge animal lover and activist and lover of mother nature. She is dedicated to preserving our beautiful planet.

Linda Somers is a Meteorologist and was a model for over 25 years and now sings in her band called Honey Bee. She is completely dedicated to volunteering her time, with a group she started to help her fellow Floridians, thru severe weather and Hurricanes.

Find on Facebook @Florida Severe Weather and @Honey Bee.

www.ingramcontent.com/pod-product-compliance
Lightning Source LLC
Chambersburg PA
CBHW071132280326
41935CB00010B/1196